Cooking
ABOARD YOUR RV

Good Food in Less Time—More than 300 Recipes and Tips

Janet Groene

Ragged Mountain Press / McGraw-Hill

Camden, Maine ◆ New York ◆ Chicago ◆ San Francisco ◆ Lisbon ◆
London ◆ Madrid ◆ Mexico City ◆ Milan ◆
Seoul ◆ Singapore ◆ Sydney

To Mom, who proofread and prodded,

tested and suggested, spelled and smelled, tasted

and taught. And to Gordon, who, by being there,

makes my every meal a banquet.

The **McGraw·Hill** Companies

1 2 3 4 5 6 7 8 9 0 DOC DOC 0 9 8 7 6 5 4

© 2004 by Ragged Mountain Press
All rights reserved. The publisher takes no responsibility for the use of any of the materials or methods described in this book, nor for the products thereof. The name "Ragged Mountain Press" and the Ragged Mountain Press logo are trademarks of The McGraw-Hill Companies. Printed in the United States of America.

Library of Congress Cataloging-in-Publication Data
Groene, Janet.
    Cooking aboard your RV / Janet Groene.— 2nd ed.
        p.   cm.
Includes index.
    ISBN 0-07-143239-6 (pbk.)
    1. Cookery. 2. Recreational vehicle living. 3. Camping.
    I. Title.
    TX840.M6G76 2004
    641.5′75—dc22   2003026859

Questions regarding the content of this book should be addressed to
Ragged Mountain Press
P.O. Box 220
Camden, ME 04843
www.raggedmountainpress.com

Questions regarding the ordering of this book should be addressed to
The McGraw-Hill Companies
Customer Service Department
P.O. Box 547
Blacklick, OH 43004
Retail customers: 1-800-262-4729
Bookstores: 1-800-722-4726

Some of these recipes appeared previously in *Family Motor Coaching* magazine and are reprinted here with permission.

Photo on title page courtesy David Stoecklein/Corbis.

Contents

Preface to the Second Edition

The first edition of *Cooking Aboard Your RV* came out in 1993. Why a new edition now? RVs are still the same "freedom machines" they have always been, and this secret has been discovered by a younger, more active generation. Retirees still like the RV life, often living aboard and traveling as a full-time way of life, but the RV lifestyle has also caught on with young singles, couples, and families with a wide spectrum of interests. Some want only a comfortable second home they can park anywhere on weekends and vacations. Others sell the house and furniture, pack up the kids, and hit the road, home-schooling the children and finding jobs along the way. They may live and travel in the RV for months and even years.

As for their homes on wheels, RVs are roomier than ever. They probably have home theaters, computer stations, and wireless access to all the electronics of our age, from communications to games. While today's galley has a larger refrigerator and freezer than RVs had in the 1990s, its stove is smaller, probably a two-burner cooktop plus a microwave-convection oven. Faced with this strange blending of heat and microwaves, many RV cooks are baffled. So this book unravels the mysteries of these space-saving combination units. As RV campers, we still love our campfire sing-alongs and marshmallow roasts. Some of us still cook on an open fire; most of us carry grills and cook outdoors as often as possible. Many of us are traditional cooks, content with our familiar comfort foods. Others love trying new ingredients, flavor combinations, and cooking techniques. And still others eat nothing but take-out and convenience foods. Full-timers have to deal with budgets and diets day in and day out. On weekends and vacations, however, RVers can take a more casual attitude toward costs and calories. In this new edition, there's something for everyone.

Janet Groene (say GRAYnee)
janetgroene@yahoo.com
2004

Weights and Measures

Weight
1 ounce = 28.35 grams
1 pound = 16 ounces = 453.6 grams
2.2 pounds = 1 kilogram

Volume
1 teaspoon = 5 milliliters
1 tablespoon = 3 teaspoons = 15 milliliters
1 fluid ounce = 6 teaspoons = $\frac{1}{8}$ cup = 29.56 milliliters
1 cup = 16 tablespoons = 8 fluid ounces = 236 milliliters
1 pint = 16 fluid ounces = 2 cups = 0.5 liter
1 quart = 32 fluid ounces = 2 pints = 0.9 liter
1 gallon = 128 fluid ounces = 4 quarts = 3.8 liters

Length
1 inch = 2.54 centimeters

Thermometer
To convert:
(°F–32) x 0.555 = °C
(°C x 1.8) + 32 = °F

slow oven = 300–325°F (150–165°C)
medium oven = 350–375°F (175–185°C)
hot oven = 400–425°F (205–220°C)

Introduction

Modern RVs have many luxuries that were unheard of in campgrounds a generation ago. We have microwave-convection ovens (see chapter 2), household refrigerators that dispense ice and water, Corian countertops, and sophisticated water-treatment systems. Some appliances may be in miniature, but we have all the comforts of home and then some.

Most of us carry small appliances, sometimes a different inventory each trip. This time we'll need a blender for smoothies, a food processor and a bread maker; next time the corn popper, George Foreman grill, and waffle maker. A toaster? Espresso maker? Deep fryer? We all have our lists of must-have, some-time, and once-in-a-blue-moon special appliances. We have 110-volt power at least part of the time and more of us are going all-electric. Those who do not want to rely solely on generator or shore power can do things with propane and 12-volt power that kitchen cooks can't.

What we usually do *not* have are a garbage disposal (it could create plumbing problems in an RV), trash compacter, unlimited water, full-size stoves and ovens with broilers, enough cupboard or counter space, a freezer big enough for half a steer, a maple chopping block, or any of the bulky, single-purpose appliances we might have in a farmhouse kitchen at home.

In this book, I'll celebrate the many conveniences that modern RVs offer but, as an active RV traveler, I will also remember the problems and limitations of RV cooking.

Among my personal peeves are recipes for "one-dish" meals that require many pans and bowls before they end up in one pot, "quick" recipes that start with a step that takes hours ("boil and pick meat from one bushel blue crabs"), fancy recipes that call for exotic ingredients I'm unlikely to carry aboard, and dishes that require great quantities of water for cooking or rinsing.

If you're like me, you want recipes for foods that are good to eat and to look at, healthful and nutritious, fairly quick and easy to cook without making undue mess, and recipes that mesh with the casual, active, chic, and health-conscious outdoor lifestyle.

In presenting my recipes and instructions, I'm assuming that you already know the basics of cooking. I didn't want to take up space with lengthy explanations of how to test for doneness, how to hard-boil eggs, or how to cut shortening into dry ingredients. If cooking terms are new to you, get any good, basic cookbook, such as the *Joy of Cooking, Betty Crocker's Cookbook,* or *The Good Housekeeping Illustrated Cookbook.*

Writing a book for the RV cook is a tall order because we are all different. I know many RV families who love to gather around the campfire and cook as they did in their tenting days. Some want quick recipes that are ready to serve in minutes. Others prefer slow, fragrant soups and stews that cook all day in an oven or in a Dutch oven buried in campfire coals while the family climbs, hikes, dives, plays tennis, or explores a cave.

Some RV cooks are classic cordon bleu chefs, maintaining the highest cuisine standards. (One of my friends carries a set of crystal wine glasses that cost about $60 per stem.) Others couldn't care less about food. They'd rather live on apples and peanut butter and spend their time reading or playing.

Some RV campers are vegetarians, diabetics, or weight watchers. Some are brawny, athletic types who need more calories in a day than others consume in a week. Some have finicky or allergic kids. Some live off the land. Some live on canned ravioli and frozen pizza. Some insist on carrying a clay cooking pot or automatic steam cooker or electric potato peeler—items that most of us never use, even at home.

Despite our differences, all of us eat. And to most of us the preparing and sharing of mealtimes is one of the most rewarding and unifying of campground pleasures. In remembering our sameness and respecting our differences, I hope I've assembled a collection of recipes that will work for most RV travelers most of the time.

One

How Green Was My Galley

In the pecking order that environmental purists create for themselves, RV camping usually comes in close to the bottom because we are perceived as luxury-loving sissies who bring all our conveniences to the wilderness with us.

Let's look at some of our good points. For one thing, we cook "from scratch" more than other campers do (meaning we discard less packaging and trash) and we bring more of our own facilities, including clean-burning propane or electric cookers. While we're traveling in our RVs, we are living in miniature. Meanwhile, the air conditioner, furnace, water heater, self-cleaning oven, automatic dishwasher, garbage disposal, and other appliances at home are turned off.

It's our outdoors too, so we are as careful as any other campers about recycling, waste disposal, and water conservation.

In many cases, we are using fewer campground resources. We are providing much of our own energy in the form of generator power, 12-volt battery power (some of which is often provided by roof-mounted solar panels), and propane. We may bring in some or all of our own water and take out some or all of our own wastewater.

Many "primitive" campers plug into campground power to run their electric blankets, hot plates, heaters, corn poppers, and lights. We RVers, by contrast, know the price of energy because we have to charge our own batteries, refill our own propane tanks, and fuel and maintain our own generators.

Because most of us have brought all our own facilities with us, we don't ask the park to provide us with hot showers, firewood, grills, and flush toilets. If we do play a television or stereo, we can close the doors and windows so others don't have to listen to our choice of program, unlike those who sleep under the stars and inflict their boom boxes and smoky fires on everyone.

It's true that some RV campers are slobs, just as some tenters and some backpackers are slobs. But RV campers have made a big dollar investment in their units, far more than has to be made in any other form of camping, which makes us deeply concerned about the preservation of our camping resources. We're in for the long haul and have put our money where our mouth is.

We *can* take it with us. That means we can also pack much of it *out* with us rather than burning, burying, or leaving our trash for the rangers to haul away.

Here are some ways to make your RV cooking style even more conservation conscious.

◆ Try a pressure cooker. It's a great energy saver and in many cases is quicker than a microwave. It uses less fuel and, because cooking times are shorter, puts less burden on the air conditioning.

◆ Carry powdered and concentrated drink mixes and reconstitute them in reusable containers. Don't carry bottled juices and canned sodas. Why transport heavy, disposable containers filled with what is essentially water?

◆ Install a good water treatment system in the RV, and you'll have safe drinking water anywhere you go without having to lug along bottled water.

◆ Long-life (UHT) milk in cardboard cartons leaves less waste than a plastic bottle. Powdered milk is the most compact of all, leaving the least trash. The secret to making it palatable is to mix it two to three hours before drinking it. Because protein is reluctant to combine with water, "steeping" time, in addition to thorough chilling, is needed to eliminate the chalky texture of reconstituted milk.

◆ If you must use foods that come in bulky packaging, repackage them at home in reusable containers—crackers and cookies into tin boxes, cereals and grains into glass or plastic jars. Such containers also help preserve freshness.

◆ Use nature's packaging: whole fresh fruits and vegetables; garlic by the braid; nuts in the shell; sausages and cheeses in natural casings; real eggs in real shells; and whole grains.

◆ When you buy produce in plastic net bags, save the bags to use as scrubbers. They are as effective as steel wool but won't scratch delicate surfaces like nonstick pan coatings. Plastic net is also good for scrubbing bugs off the nose of the RV.

◆ Don't use steel wool or cleansers that could leave a gritty residue. When you're skimping on water, a lengthy rinse isn't always possible.

◆ In drought areas where your gray water might save a tree, use it as allowed to water worthy plants. Water used to cook pasta, rinse sprouts, wash greens, or boil eggs can be drained from the pot into the dishpan and used as part of the wash-up water. Don't dump salty, soapy, or spiced water on the ground. It could damage plants.

◆ Buy only environmentally responsible RV chemicals. Baking soda is an effective, food-quality galley cleanser. Vinegar or ammonia, mixed in a water solution, makes glass sparkle. A cut lemon dipped in salt cleans copper. Soft soap rubbed on the outside of a cooking pot before it's put over the fire can be washed off later, taking campfire carbon with it.

◆ Minimize the use of chemical sprays by making maximum use of flypaper and screens.

◆ Don't use toilet chemicals that contain formaldehyde, or non-potable antifreezes in drinking water tanks.

◆ Instead of buying small sizes for galley use, save small containers at home to make up weekend-size portions of galley staples.

◆ Where possible, buy or repackage spreadables such as peanut butter, margarine, mustard, ketchup, mayonnaise, and jelly in squeeze containers. It's more sanitary to squeeze them onto the bread, and you won't have to wash extra spreaders and spoons.

◆ "Old-fashioned" basic ingredients are almost always the most nutritious and compact, with the least packaging. Bring plain pop-corn, not fancy packaged types. Snack on freshly popped corn in-stead of greasy, bulky potato chips. European-style crisp breads are preferable to snack crackers. They come in simple paper wrappers instead of bulky boxes with plastic liners and contain little or no fat. You can carry a serving of rolled oats or other to-be-cooked ce-real in a fraction of the space taken by ready-to-eat cereals. A sim-ple sack of uncooked rice will feed an army.

◆ Invest in plastic egg carriers, sold in camp supply stores. Buy eggs in bulk, not in puffy plastic containers, and carry them safely in these reusable cases.

◆ Buy cookware with the best and most durable nonstick coatings. In many cases, no dishwashing is required. They wipe clean with a paper towel.

◆ Start a collection at home of freshly laundered rags, preferably linen or cotton. When folding and sorting laundry, I take out any towel, sheet, or other natural-fiber item that is good for one more use as a rag, and put it into a clean sack consigned to the camper. Instead of reaching for a paper towel, I reach for a clean rag. When it's soiled, it becomes biodegradable trash.

◆ Disposables are a way of life in camping but they add cost, bulk, and trash problems to the trip. Cut down on paper cups by buying an individualized mug for each member of the family. Make every-one responsible for rinsing out their own mugs after each use and returning them to the cupboard.

◆ Use insulated containers to keep things cold or hot. Fill an ice bucket with ice cubes for cocktail hour so the refrigerator door doesn't have to be opened repeatedly. Fill a thermos with coffee or hot water. Use natural coolers (e.g., put the six-pack in the stream) and heaters. (The dashboard becomes a greenhouse when the sun is shining in. Set the yogurt or raise the bread dough there.)

◆ The most effective bleach for natural fibers, especially linen, is sunshine. Dry dishcloths and dishtowels in the sun.

◆ Read labels. Most of us use far more of every detergent, cleaner, and chemical than required.

◆ Make an awning or sunshade for the area where the refrigerator coils are so the unit won't have to work unnecessarily hard.

◆ It probably isn't necessary to leave the water heater on all the time in camp. Most RVs have a small quick-recovery unit that can be turned on only as needed for showers and dishwashing.

◆ Invest in a solar battery charger. It's a silent servant, working unseen on the RV roof. The more panels you can afford, the longer you can linger in the wilderness without starting the engine or generator.

◆ Minimize your dependence on an AC generator as much as possible. Generators cost money to buy, fuel, and maintain, and they generate fumes and noise. Many galley appliances can be found in 12-volt versions; others, such as Nordic Ware's waffle maker and Coleman's coffeemaker, are available in stovetop models that operate atop the gas stove; still others can be run off your 12-volt "house" battery system through an inverter. Even a microwave oven can be run off an inverter *if* you have a large enough inverter and a big enough battery bank to supply it.

◆ Learn about fireless cookers. Various commercial models are available through camping supply stores, or make your own by using an ice chest filled with newspapers, pillows, or straw pallets, leaving just a small space for a pot. Insulation must be many inches thick and must surround the pot tightly. Bring a heavy pot of stew or soaked beans to a full boil, cover tightly, quickly place it in a fireless cooker, and don't peek all day. Six to eight hours later it's cooked to perfection.

◆ Experiment with manifold cooking, in which foil-wrapped foods cook in surplus engine heat underway. It all depends on the size and shape of spaces you have available under the hood, and what temperatures are maintained there, so some experimenting will be needed before you perfect the pot roast recipe that will work on *your* engine, in the space available in *your* engine compartment, in the length of time it takes to get where you're going.

◆ Surplus engine heat can also be channeled to the water heater in some RVs. The system is used more commonly on boats, so you might ask a marine center about the feasibility of using a similar heat exchanger in your RV.

◆ Grow your own sprouts and you'll have fresh, natural greens everywhere you go. Because a tablespoon or two of seeds swells to a quart of sprouts in a few days, you can carry an entire produce patch in a few ounces of weight.

◆ Everything you carry in your RV costs petrodollars to accelerate, cruise, and brake. Buy everything possible in a powdered, dehydrated, concentrated, dried, boneless, or compressed form. If it comes in both glass and plastic (liquor, wine, mustard, vinegar, sodas, mayo), plastic is lighter and less breakable.

◆ Think in terms of portions per pound and per cubic inch. You can feed four to six with a tiny jar of dried chipped beef or a 12-ounce can of corned beef and a lot of white sauce, feed twelve with a pound of rice and enough fillers, and feed multitudes with a pound of popcorn.

◆ Although individual packaging costs more and makes for more trash, it has a place in your RV camp-out. Individual packets save work, time, and waste. They control portions for you (how many bowls of cereal can you get from a 17-ounce box?), and they keep every morsel fresh until the package is opened. In some cases, it's a wise trade-off.

◆ Pay heed to fire laws in each campground. They vary according to area and season. Where fires are allowed, stick to wood, cardboard, and paper. Don't burn plastics, foils, or garbage. An electric charcoal-fire starter is safer than petroleum-based charcoal starters, and pollutes the air less.

◆ Recycling practices are different in every community. Separate recyclables in the way that is best for *this* campground or community. It may be quite different from the way you sort things at home.

◆ If you have a choice when purchasing a new RV, or can convert your present one, get a stove hood that has an overboard exhaust rather than a recirculating filter. Filters are only moderately effective on odors and spatters, and they don't remove moisture or heat at all, so your air conditioner works harder.

◆ Where you have filters that can be washed or changed, be scrupulous about it. Don't forget the air conditioners (both automotive and rooftop), stove exhaust, furnace, and vacuum cleaner. Clogged filters cost energy.

◆ Don't use drain cleaners. They could damage the RV's plumbing or tanks, and they add chemicals to the environment. Fit all drains with good basket strainers. When stoppages occur, clear them with a plumber's helper.

◆ Use rechargeable batteries and rechargeable appliances.

◆ Use pump- and spray-type soaps and cleaners that can be refilled.

For more helpful galley hints, see Miscellaneous Tips in the appendix.

About Living Off the Land

Trying native foods is one of the most exciting and interesting ways for serious travelers to enjoy different regions to the fullest. Stopping at roadside stands is more than a shopping experience. It's an opportunity to meet local people, discover new foods, and to learn from experts how to prepare them.

Gleaning is another way to live off the land, when farmers invite people into their fields after the harvest to take whatever leavings they can find. By the end of a season's camping in North Carolina, we had cupboards filled with canned and dried apples from orchards that commercial growers had abandoned.

U-pick farms are found throughout the nation. Watch for road signs, read ads in shopper tabloids, or write each state's Department of Agriculture to see if they publish a list of such farms. Prices are not always dirt cheap, but you're able to pick the very best of the crop at its peak freshness.

In our RV we've always carried a few books about living off the land. However, as populations balloon and pressure on our wilderness increases, responsible campers are more careful about harvesting nature's bounty. In public parks it's illegal to pick anything. It's forbidden nationwide to pick sea oats, a cereal once savored.

In any case, it's irresponsible to take more than a modest share. In some places, permits are required to harvest wild edibles such as stone crabs or wild rice.

Never forget that most land belongs to someone. Poaching game, pinching watermelons from farm fields, or picking from roadside orchards and groves is *stealing*. In areas where farm families have to live all year on the proceeds of one harvest, officials are not amused by tourists who help themselves. At worst, you can pay fines totaling hundreds of thousands of dollars.

In some cases, it's too dangerous to live off the land—or sea—with its pollutants, residues, red tides, and mercury. And even experts are sometimes fooled by wild mushrooms. Proceed with full knowledge of the area, its flora and fauna, its folkways, and its current laws.

Some foods, such as pokeweed, dandelion, or cactus are so common in some areas, almost any child can identify them. Others are uncommon even in areas where they grow, so it takes a little more investigating to make sure they're safe to eat.

The best thing about regional harvests is that they give us travelers a new tool to make friends. Strike up conversations with locals, especially senior citizens. Listen to the lore of regional foods. Some, such as a regional belief that elderberries are poison, are utter nonsense. Others, such as a warning against touching a manchineel tree or even standing under one in the rain, could save you a lot of grief. And some tales are made up on the spot, I'm sure, to impress an outsider who won't know the difference anyway. The rest is pure gold, 24-carat Americana in its sweetest form.

Listen and learn, and your family's love for the land will grow and grow.

Two

Furnishing the Kitchen on Wheels

How can you feed shark-size appetites out of a minnow-size RV gal-ley? It all begins with the choice of equipment that is exactly right for the task. Not garage-sale junk. Not the stuff that isn't good enough to use in the kitchen anymore. And not thin, cheap pans with battered, ill-fitting lids.

It's tempting to furnish the RV with cast-offs but RV cookery is tricky enough without additional roadblocks. No matter how luxurious your galley, it's still a working kitchen with too little storage space, limited water, fewer conveniences than at home, and never enough countertop area. You need the right equipment in the right sizes, amounts, and materials. Nothing more, nothing less.

A basic inventory might include:

Balloon whisk. For quick mixing jobs without an electric beater, it will do a more thorough job than a spoon and is easier to wash than an egg beater. I carry a large one for batters and a tiny one for small tasks such as whisking herbs into mayo or sour cream.

Bucket. You need a scrub bucket anyway, so invest in a high-quality stainless steel pail that can also be used as a lobster or pasta pot, laundry basin, and carryall.

Can opener. Spend the extra money to get a double-geared type; both wheels turn together, transporting the can as the cut is made.

Cutting board. Get one that doubles as a sink fill-in piece to increase your counter space.

Dishes and glassware. The lighter and more breakproof, the better. Avoid heavy pottery and ironstone, which cost fuel dollars to transport, and disposables, which are expensive both to your budget and to the environment. Favor plastics or Corelle. In mugs and glasses, look for unbreakable *and* stackable. Stainless steel commuter mugs keep coffee hot for a few hours.

Ice bucket. If you get an ice bucket that can withstand hot temperatures as well as cold, you can use it for both. Keep ice cubes on hand to cut down on traffic in and out of the refrigerator. When you're cooking a meal of many courses and are short of burners, cook one dish ahead of time and keep it hot in an ice bucket.

I once met a camper who brought her potatoes to a hard boil just until they were crisp-tender, and then transferred them to an insulated container–ice bucket. The potatoes continued to simmer until they were tender and she had freed a burner to cook another course. (If you try this, use only an ice bucket that has a heat-tolerant liner.)

Ice chests. Keep separate ice chests for fish and bait and, if your family drinks a lot of canned beer or soda, another one for that. Keep the mess, smells, and traffic out of your refrigerator. When you don't need it as an ice chest, use it as a catchall. Big, box-style ice chests also serve as outdoor seats, tables, and work surfaces.

Use ice chests for hot foods, too, to carry hot take-out meals to the campground. One Kansas family stops for Chinese food on Friday nights on the way out of town in the RV. The piping-hot cartons are put in an ice chest that has been thickly lined with newspapers and preheated by placing a heated pan inside. The food is still hot and ready to eat when they reach the campsite.

Use a warm ice chest for raising dough and culturing yogurt by putting either in the chest with a bottle of very hot water. Close tightly and let the heat from the water maintain the right warmth.

Knives. Get a good, basic set of knives with a holder that will keep them safe on the road. Rattling around in a drawer will dull and nick the edges.

Measurers. Plastic measuring cups do nothing but measure. Instead, get stainless steel measuring cups, which can also be used for melting butter or heating syrup over a burner set on low. Large Pyrex measuring cups can also be used as mixing bowls, pitchers, microwave cookware, and bakeware.

Mixing bowl(s). A nest of high-quality stainless steel mixing bowls is a lifetime investment. Get at least one supersize bowl for popcorn, big salads, and big mixing jobs. When not in use, it can be used as a fruit bowl or catchall.

Mugs. Instead of spending money on disposables, get a distinctive mug for each member of the family. Each person can use and rinse his or her own mug. It will need a sudsy hot wash only once a day or so.

Pitcher. Rather than carry heavy, bulky drinks in bottles and cans, rely on juice concentrates and dry mixes such as Kool-Aid, Crystal Light, and ice tea. Mix them as needed.

Plastic crate(s). Now readily available in heavy-duty plastic in all sizes, carryalls come in rigid or folding models. They can be used in many ways. Round up all your cookout equipment in one, canned goods in another. Use them as "drawers" on an unused bunk and fill them with linens or clothing. Use them as dividers in big, cavernous holds under dinette seats and in the RV's "basement."

Use an upturned empty crate as an entry step to your RV. Dirt on your shoes will drop through the holes and onto the ground.

If you're doing dishes outdoors, give them a good sudsing, place them in a plastic crate, and hose to rinse. Then air-dry in the breeze.

Pots and pans. Consider weight, versatility, cleanability, and stackability. Iron is heavy and it rusts, but old-timers prefer it for campfire cooking. (I don't recommend it for stovetop cooking because of its poor heat-transfer qualities.) Cast aluminum is best for slow, even heat in stovetop baking and Dutch oven cooking in the campfire; stamped aluminum provides instant heat transfer for sautéing. Durotherm makes pots and casseroles in multilayer metal that holds heat so well, foods stay hot for hours at potlucks. So unusual is the cooking with these pots, they come with an instructional video. Shop specialty housewares stores or go to www.durotherm.com.

Some microware can be used in conventional ovens too, so some RV cooks carry no other bakeware. Stackable, steamer-type pots can cook three or more foods at once. Look for them in stainless steel and in microware.

A pressure cooker saves time and fuel and can be used without pressure when you need an extra saucepan. Stir-fry cooking is quick and practical; consider adding a wok. For short trips all the foods can be cut up and packaged at home, then stir-fried in a flash. Get at least one small and one large nonstick skillet in a good brand such as T-Fal. A swish of cold water and a swipe with a paper towel get them clean.

My advice is to start with one or two thick, lidded pots and a high-quality, lidded, nonstick skillet. Then add pans and microware as needed. I emphasize that the pans (except for sauté pans) should be heavy, in seeming contradiction to the appeal of lightweight galleyware, if the RV chef likes to produce multicourse meals that involve a lot of shuffling among two burners. Heavy pots hold heat better, even in cold or windy weather.

Rechargeable appliances. Consider getting a cordless electric beater so you'll have full-time electric mixing even when you're not on generator or shore power. Cordless can openers and electric knives also are available. Such appliances need regular recharging; they're not for the cook who goes long periods without AC or who uses the RV infrequently. Ours is mounted permanently, so it's always on charge when we're plugged in. Although rechargeables have come many miles since their early days, when they were quirky and underpowered, they still rely on regular recharging. Never put one away discharged and don't leave them in the RV during long layups.

Shakers. At home, wash and save large jars, such as mayonnaise jars, that have a tight seal and take them RVing to use as disposable, shake-and-pour mixing containers. Shake up pancake batter, instant pudding and smoothies. Smaller shakers are good for whipping eggs for omelets or making salad dressings. Simply dump all ingredients into the jar, screw on the lid, shake to mix, and pour. Instead of having to wash a bowl, spatula, and beater, just put a little water in the jar with some detergent and a few pebbles or a teaspoon of uncooked rice, and shake until it's scrubbed clean. Rinse and dry. If you have more than you need, just swish them out and throw them in the recycling bin.

Silverware. Two-piece tableware with plastic or wood handles is inexpensive and good looking, but germs and goo can hide in the seams. Get high-quality, seamless silverware with a smooth finish. It will clean more easily, with less water, in hand dishwashing.

Small appliances. Try to find electric appliances that do more than one thing. Toaster ovens, which can bake, broil or toast, come in many sizes and styles. Oster offers a mixer that has attachments including food processor, salad maker, juicer, and blender. Almost every RV now has a combination microwave-convection oven, often with no other oven. (For more information, see the end of this chapter.) While an electric coffeemaker is a convenience, look into Coleman's stovetop coffeemaker and you can make your morning brew without starting the generator. It works much the same as a Mr. Coffee, but atop the burner.

Thermos bottles. You can save time, trouble, and energy if you keep a container of hot water and one of ice water or ice tea on hand. When cold drinks are handy in their own containers, your family members aren't into the refrigerator every two minutes. With hot water you can make coffee, tea, bouillon, gelatin, instant cocoa, and many other treats without lighting the stove or heating a kettle of water.

The Little (and Not So Little) Luxuries

The marketplace overflows with tempting kitchen accessories and countertop appliances and I try most of them with the RV galley in mind. While every new appliance is useful to some cooks some of the time, RV cooks have to make tough choices about what to take and what to leave at home. Every holiday season seems to bring a new crop of small appliances. Many of them wind up under the tree this year, and at the garage sale next year.

Remember the doughnut-maker craze a few years ago? And the powered cookie press? Hot-air corn poppers? Deep-fat fryers? Some appliances enjoy a brief sensation, disappear, and resurface every few years. Blenders have made a big comeback recently thanks to the smoothies craze, and everyone loves tabletop electric grills. Other appliances, such as automatic bread makers, pasta makers, and espresso machines, are a passing fad in some households but become necessities in others.

Here are some considerations in choosing small appliances for the RV galley. In the end, however, the only considerations are your own cooking style, the priorities you put on your limited storage space, and the feasibility of using those appliances within the limits of space, weight, and electrical power available to you.

If you already have any of these small appliances, you might try them aboard the RV one at a time. It makes every trip's menus more interesting if you focus on homemade breads this time, deep-fry treats the next, and daily homemade sorbets after that.

I've rated these appliances electrically Low, Medium, and High. Those requiring Low or Medium power can be run, at least for short periods, on small or medium inverters; those rated High need large inverters, shore power, or generator power. Keep in mind the one drawback shared by all countertop appliances: Unless it's bolted down, it can't stay on the counter underway. It must be stowed securely each time you drive away.

Here are some appliance pros and cons.

Automatic Bread Maker

What it is: A completely automated bread "factory" in which you place all the ingredients. About two hours later, a perfect loaf of bread is turned out.

Pros: Because a daily supply of fresh bread is one of camping's biggest shopping problems, this allows an unending supply of fresh and fragrant "staff of life." Because high-quality bakery bread is difficult to find when you're on the go, this provides a healthy alternative to white fluff.

Cons: Heavy for its size. Requires Medium-High AC. Computer operated, so any AC interruption stops the cycle and requires manual completion of the loaf. Makes only one loaf at a time; not practical for larger families.

Blender

What it is: A tiny, very high speed blade pulverizes food and ice.

Pros: Small size, available in a powerful 12-volt model. Modest AC needs allow 110-volt models to be used on most inverters. Invaluable for making frozen drinks, health drinks, purees, baby food. Easy to clean.

Cons: Cannot whip cream or egg whites. Limited uses. Some cooks find the food processor does most things they used to do with a blender, and more.

Coffemaker

What it is: The automatic coffeemaker rates second only to the toaster as the most essential item in many kitchens.

Pros: Convenient. Available for permanent, under-counter installation.

Cons: Medium-High AC needs. Programmable models not practical unless you have full-time AC. Not multipurpose; only makes coffee. Ground coffee is less compact to carry than instant. Note that Coleman makes a stovetop version that requires no electricity.

Deep Fryer

What it is: The new models cook with less mess and less fat to make homemade doughnuts, french fries, fritters, and much more.

Pros: If your family demands a lot of fried foods, you can cook with more healthful ingredients if you make your own. Quick and convenient. Some models combine frying with pressure to make fast-food-style chicken and fish. Fresh doughnuts or french fries are a great attention-getter in campgrounds.

Cons: Comparatively heavy. Messy. Medium-High AC needs. Limited uses. Cooking oil is expensive; filtering and saving oil for reuse is cumbersome, and used oil may require special disposal in campgrounds.

Electric Skillet

What it is: A thermostat-controlled electric frying pan.

Pros: Available in many sizes, from miniatures that can fry a couple of eggs to large fryer-roasters with domed lids. Can be used to bake, fry, or braise. Available in both 110- and 12-volt models.

Cons: High AC needs. Can only bake, fry, or braise. If, on the other hand, you carry an electric buffet burner (hot plate), you have a thermostat-controlled cooker that can be used under a coffeemaker, corn popper, tea kettle, skillet, saucepan, griddle, double boiler, Dutch oven, stovetop toaster, wok, or pressure cooker. In short, the electric skillet is an extra burner with limited abilities, so why not add an extra electric burner in the form of a hot plate?

Food Processor

What it is: Full-feature models have a knife blade to mince and grind, a paddle for mixing, and two or more cutting wheels that shred and grate. Small and battery models have very limited uses, such as chopping parsley.

Pros: A necessity to many modern cooks. Modest AC needs, many uses.

Cons: Not easy to clean. Comparatively heavy.

Ice-Cream Maker

What it is: Makes homemade ice cream, sherbet, sorbet.

Pros: Allows you to favor more healthful ingredients and eliminate chemical additives. Many types available, from hand-crank models to fully automatic appliances that are placed inside the freezer. Electric models require Low AC. A great team sport in camp.

Cons: Bulky and most types are hard to clean. Ingredients are bulky too, although some are available in powdered form. When salt is used, resulting runoff is very corrosive and not good for nearby trees and plants.

Juicer

What it is: An appliance that reduces whole fresh fruits and vegetables to juice.

Pros: Very popular with people who are sold on "juicing" as a healthful diet. Extracts more nutrients from foods than do juicer attachments.

Cons: Medium AC requirement. Comparatively heavy. Limited uses unless you're on a juice diet. Hard to clean. Some foods require peeling first.

Kitchen Wand

What it is: Its high-speed, blender-type blade can be used to whip and chop in any container you choose. Popular in Europe and indispensable to many professional chefs.

Pros: Very light, compact, versatile. Low AC draw or rechargeable. Easy to clean; can be used in a disposable jar or cup. Inexpensive.

Cons: Requires a lot of practice to wield one like professional demonstrators do.

Sandwich Maker

What it is: A modern version of the old campfire pie iron, these new electric appliances have a nonstick lining that allows messless cooking of filled sandwiches and pastries.

Pros: Small, lightweight, wipes clean with a damp cloth. It is fun to invent new fillings and wrappers. Can be used for breakfast, lunch, desserts, snacks. Nonelectric stovetop models with nonstick finish are available.

Cons: Requires Medium-High AC. Limited versatility. Small size makes them impractical for large families.

Tabletop Grill

What it is: An electric grill for broiling meat, fish, or vegetables. The cooking surface is slanted so excess fat drains into a reservoir.

Pros: Because the broilers in most RV ovens are small and ineffective, an alternate method of indoor grilling is always welcome. Can be used indoors or out. Available in many sizes for small or large families. Lightweight. A clean, quick, and convenient alternative to charcoal.

Cons: Messy to clean despite very slick nonstick lining. Take a big supply of rags or newspaper. High AC requirement. Bulky. Not versatile; does nothing but grill.

Toaster Oven

What it is: An automatic toaster that also can also be used for baking and broiling.

Pros: Many sizes and models are available. Smaller ones are no larger than a pop-up, two-slice toaster, yet can toast bread and bagels, as well as bake potatoes or a small meatloaf. Larger ones can be used to roast a whole chicken. Comparatively lightweight. Available with continuous-clean interiors, and under-counter models can be permanently installed in the RV.

Cons: High AC draw. Limited capacity.

Vacuum Sealer

What it is: A compact device that evacuates air out of food packaging. Mine is the Tilia FoodSaver. It's used with special plastic bags that can go from the freezer to a pot of boiling water. Cook double amounts at home, freeze for RV trips, and you might go through an entire RV vacation without having to cook or wash a pot! Storage times (see appendix) are doubled or tripled when foods are stored in a vacuum.

Pros: Can be kept at home and only used to prepare food for RV trips, but also compact enough to carry along mounted on a wall or stowed in a cupboard. Quickly and easily seals any food for the shelf, refrigerator, or freezer. Virtually any food (including fresh fruits and vegetables carried in the refrigerator) will keep longer when air is removed. Foods can be warmed or cooked in the same bag. Vacuum-sealed gorp will stay fresh and moisture-free on the trail. Also available is a Tilia model that evacuates air from canning jars, creating bugproof storage in reusable jars.

Cons: Requires Medium AC. Bags can be reused several times but cost more than regular plastic bags.

The New RV Galley

Luc Van Herle, product planning manager for Fleetwood Enterprises, and Patrick F. Carroll, vice president of product development at Monaco Coach Corporation, allowed me to look into their crystal balls to see the RV galley of 2005 and beyond. "We're now in the long-promised transition to a market composed chiefly of baby boomers," reveals Van Herle. "Their RV usages and expectations are completely different. At one time, RVing was a lifestyle that took place in the campground. Today's buyer may use the RV only as a support vehicle for another lifestyle. A family might, for example, use the motorhome to tow a trailer of ATVs and spend the day at the dunes. Or a family goes to the dog show, the ski slopes, or a lake where everyone goes waterskiing."

Of course, you'll always be able to order the RV galley layout of your dreams, but it may be far different from the galley you thought you had to settle for. Galleys of today and tomorrow are more and more residential in every surface, appliance, and convenience—even to full-featured household refrigerators that work only on 110-volt household power. "Go to a design center or home show. What's hot there is what's hot in RV living," says Van Herle. "Galleys are getting smaller because today's families would rather devote more space to a home theater." Yet he sees tomorrow's RV as having one and a half, even two complete galleys—one indoors and the other under the awning, where a small refrigerator, barbecue, entertainment center, and perhaps a sink, slide out of the basement.

"When we introduced the two-burner stove in our motorhomes, we were almost tarred and feathered," Van Herle recalls. "Today we can't give away a conventional stove. People want a couple of burners and a microwave-convection oven, period. Countertop appliances are out, too. There are just too many choices, so we install a lot of outlets and people can choose for themselves what kind of coffeemaker to buy or whether they want a toaster oven or pop-up. We don't sell a motorhome without a generator. People want more household appliances, more battery banks, larger inverters."

Dishwashers continue to be unpopular because of the space they take up, but a drawer-style dishwasher from New Zealand is catching on with many Fleetwood buyers, says Van Herle.

Pat Carroll is known for the "Ladies Only" seminars he conducts at RV shows and rallies. Women talk about what they want in a motorcoach and he listens. He, too, finds less interest today in conventional propane stoves. Of course, Carroll reassures us, they are available to full-timers and other cooks who want three or four burners and a gas oven in addition to a microwave-convection oven.

Buyers at Monaco want elegance and are willing to pay it. One option is a $1,200 water system that treats water, then adds ozone for the utmost purity. Unlike Van Herle, who sees a trend to outdoor dining, Carroll finds that most Monaco buyers prefer to eat indoors in bug-free, climate-controlled comfort. When RVs are built with three and four slide-outs, as most are, that means a loss of "basement" space, he finds.

Like Van Herle, Carroll sees a big pullback in the addition of small appliances to the galley at the factory. "We just can't second-guess customers," he admits. With such a profusion of models on the market, he finds it best to leave counters empty and let buyers decide for themselves about a toaster, blender, cappuccino maker, food processor, waffle iron, bread maker, and so on. Part-timers may want to carry different appliances on different trips; full-timers can decide what appliances they'll use most. The built-in coffeemaker that was almost standard a few years ago is no longer taken for granted.

The coach of tomorrow will be more comfortable, more durable, and more spacious than ever before. Keeping in mind the wide range of appetites, cooking styles, and interests of RVers, the recipes in this book were chosen to work for most RV chefs most of the time. There has never been a better time to have an RV for traveling and dining in style.

Mastering the Microwave-Convection Oven

The good news is that the combination microwave-convection oven isn't nearly as daunting at it may appear at first. It's an ordinary microwave and an ordinary oven. The word *convection* simply means the transfer of heat, so you can simply set the oven temperature at 350 or 425°F as you have always done. Because the oven has a fan to distribute heat better, it may cook a little faster or more evenly than other ovens. But every oven has its quirks and you'll soon get used to this one.

If you use it as a microwave or regular oven, you never need to stray into the briarpatch of combination, or Combo, cooking. For regular baking or roasting in any recipe, use the convection oven with its familiar time and temperature settings. For microwaving any recipe, choose the same times and power settings called for, allowing for differences in wattage.

Confusion often occurs when using the Auto-Combi, or Combo, feature. Here's why. Every micro-convection oven is different by nature according to its power and size. When you get into combination cooking, which means setting the oven to produce heat and microwaves at the same time, brands differ in their terms, times, programming, and capabilities. The directions that come with one brand of combination oven won't work with most other brands and, if you get recipes from your friends, they may call for steps or settings that make no sense on your oven's touchpad.

My own microwave-convection oven is made by Dometic, a popular RV appliance brand. It's an over-the-stove model with overboard venting. Other brands popular with RV manufacturers include Sharp and GE. Countertop and over-the-range combination ovens are available, some with overboard exhaust and others with recirculating filters. Others are built in under the counter, at the level where you'd find a conventional oven.

Some general observations:

◆ Convection ovens produce heat, which means that grime builds up and bakes on the same as gas or electric conventional ovens. The less you use your combination oven in convection mode, the easier it is to keep clean.

◆ A convection oven is simply a hot oven with a fan in it. Because the hot air circulates more effectively, you might try temperatures about 25°F lower than those called for in conventional ovens. Cooking times may also be shorter. Every oven, including the traditional RV gas oven, has idiosyncracies. Until you get used to them, keep a closer eye on the oven as you bake.

◆ Convection baking calls for preheating the oven, just as with any other oven that cooks with heat. It's also best to start most Combo cooking in a preheated oven. Some models incorporate this step into an auto-cook cycle.

◆ Don't risk an expensive steak or roast in a Combo mode until you know its capabilities. Try broiling burgers or baking a meatloaf to see if Combo meat cookery is for you. I've had excellent results Combo-roasting poultry and meats suitable for braising, such as pot roast or barbecued pork, using a roasting bag according to manufacturer directions and cooking times provided by my oven manufacturer. Expensive roasts, however, are best cooked the conventional way in convection mode.

◆ Invest in an instant-read thermometer. The only way to assure safe doneness of foods such as pork and poultry is by temperature.

◆ Read manufacturer directions about when and where to use oven racks for combination or convection cooking. Never use the metal rack for microwave-only cooking. Never bake or Combo cook *without* a rack.

◆ Microwaving is known for creating pops and spatters, so cooks know the importance of covering almost anything that is being nuked. In Combo cooking, in which both microwaves and heat are used, it's very possible that foods will spatter but the oven is also hot, which means you can't cover food with the papers and wraps used with microwaving alone. Use roasting bags, Teflon cooking paper, or oven-safe microware with lids.

◆ Shop for special plastic microware that can be used in a regular oven, too. Many of the new plastic baking pans can be used at temperatures up to 400°F. Corelle and Pyrex are always safe in your combination oven, too. Corelle offers a very attractive bake-and-serve line that can be seen at www.corelle.com. Pyrex measuring cups are multiuse gadgets that measure and pour, and can serve as both a mixing bowl and a microwave-safe baking container. CorningWare is a classic that goes from oven or microwave to table. (See the latest patterns at www.worldkitchen.com.)

◆ In a convection or conventional oven, it takes about the same time to bake two pies as one. However, in microwave cooking, more food takes more time; e.g., one baked potato takes 4 to 5 minutes and four baked potatoes take 16 to 20 minutes. Times for Combo cooking are also based on the amount of food in the recipe. If you double or halve the recipe, times must be increased or decreased. A 4-pound chicken will take longer than a 3-pound chicken.

◆ In my experience, Combo cooking is more trouble than it's worth. It requires more watching and takes almost as long as conventional baking. For example, a 2-pound pot roast takes 90 to 100 minutes when Combo-cooked in a glass casserole, and the meat has to be turned halfway through cooking. In a pressure cooker, the roast would be done in half the time. Meatballs require 12 to 14 minutes of High Combo cooking before they are drained, sauced, and cooked for another 10 minutes on Low Combo. Brownies need up to 15 minutes in Combo cooking, a savings of only a few minutes over convection baking. One exception is apple pie, which develops a nicely browned crust with tender apples inside in only 25 to 30 minutes of Combo cooking on High. Even a frozen pie can be put in the oven at 400°F on Combo Roast/High Mix and be done in half an hour, give or take a few minutes.

◆ If you do a lot of cooking from scratch and want to increase your microwave and combination repertoire, the undisputed mistress of this mode of cooking is Janet Sedlack. For information about her spiral-bound booklet of Combo recipes, contact her at: P.O. Box 1283, Burnsville, MN 55337; 800-784-0573; janet@microwave connect.com. (Have a credit card ready.)

Note: *Any recipe in this book that calls for an oven can be baked in a preheated convection oven set at the temperature given or up to 25°F lower.*

Three

Beverages: Let's Drink to RV Camping!

Root Beer Float

This is one of my favorite quick desserts because it can be made rich and regal with Ben and Jerry's ice cream, or dietetic using sugar-free root beer and sugar-free, fat-free frozen yogurt. If someone in your family is diabetic, here's one dessert that can be made for everyone!

8 to 12 ounces root beer per person
1 scoop vanilla ice cream per person

Put a scoop of ice cream in a tall glass, and fill the glass with root beer. (Watch it! It foams a lot.) Add a straw and a spoon, and voilà!

Block ice is often available at campgrounds. When you want to make a punch bowl for a hot day, set a block of ice on the end of the picnic table or somewhere it can drip. Chip a little depression in the top and set a metal pan or bowl in it. Fill the bowl with hot water, and keep refilling until it melts a bowl-shaped depression in the ice. Fill your solid-ice punch bowl with your favorite drink recipe and ladle into cups.

Stir $1/2$ teaspoon of your favorite flavor gelatin into a mug of hot tea. Or make a hot fruit drink with hot water and 1 teaspoon gelatin mix.

Eggnog

Until scientists can find out why some eggs already contain harmful organisms at the time they are laid, it's best not to use raw eggs in eggnog, Caesar salad, and all the other wonderful recipes that contain raw eggs. Many food-service professionals now use pasteurized eggs; cooking kills the harmful elements. For a low-fat nog, substitute a carton of egg whites and a drop of yellow food coloring.

Here's a safe way to enjoy warming, nourishing eggnog as an afternoon snack, bedtime drink, or dessert on a cold day.

5 cups milk
1 cup liquid egg substitute
$1/2$ cup sugar
1 teaspoon vanilla
dash nutmeg
rum or brandy

Heat milk over a medium flame, stirring in sugar and egg substitute until mixture is hot and somewhat thickened. Remove from heat and stir in vanilla. Serve warm with rum, kirsch, or brandy, if you like. Or chill, then thin with additional cold milk just before serving. Hot or cold, garnish with a dash of nutmeg. Makes 6 cups.

Discover nonfat powdered milk when fresh milk supplies run low. The secret to reconstituting it is to allow at least two to three hours in the refrigerator, not only to chill it but to allow time for reluctant proteins to combine fully with the water.

Posset

Far from home and feeling poorly? Here's a posset like Grandmother used to make. It will transport you back to the comforts of loved ones and home.

1 cup milk
2 teaspoons sugar
few grains salt
few drops almond flavoring

Heat milk to steaming, remove from heat, and stir in salt and sugar until they dissolve. Add almond extract, stir, and serve hot. Serves 1.

Variation: Use vanilla extract, or a drop of vanilla and a drop of almond.

Slush

This makes a fun and attractive dessert after a big meal, and it can be made with sugared or sugar-free (e.g., Crystal Light) drink mix.

1 bag crushed ice
1 packet powdered drink mix, any fruit flavor
fresh strawberries for garnish

Send a team to the camp store for a bag of crushed ice and knock it around a bit to loosen it. Pack supersize glasses or paper cups with ice. Make up powdered drink mix using only half as much water as it calls for and pour over ice. Serve with straws.

> To make crushed ice, put cubes in a clean pillowcase and pound with a hammer.

beverages

Turkish Buttermilk

If you like the taste of buttermilk, you'll like this icy and energizing bracer.

16 ounces nonfat plain yogurt
2 cups water
garlic salt to taste

Whisk everything together in a pitcher and chill thoroughly. Shake or stir again before serving. Makes 4 cups.

Your Own Chocolate Malt Mix

1 cup sugar or equivalent sugar substitute
$1/2$ cup unsweetened cocoa powder
dash salt
$1/3$ cup cold water
$1/2$ cup malted milk

Make a smooth paste of all the ingredients and bring to a boil in a heavy saucepan over very low flame or in the microwave. Take care not to burn it. Cool and store in the refrigerator. To prepare, add a teaspoon or two of the mixture to a cup of very hot milk and stir well. Makes $1\frac{1}{2}$ cups mix.

Other Beverage Ideas

◆ Carry a few mini-size liqueurs of your favorite brand, and add half a bottle to a mug of coffee for a sweet, satisfying, easy dessert.

◆ For a change, use mulling spices with cranberry or pineapple juice instead of apple juice or cider. Serve hot in mugs.

Four

Wake-Up Call: Breakfast

A t home, even with the help of countertop appliances, it's quite a jug-gling act to get toast, bacon, eggs, and coffee hot and ready at the same time. In the RV galley, with too few burners and perhaps no extra appliances at all, it's even tougher. Here are some recipes that depart from the toast-eggs-bacon habit, to make cooking easier and breakfast more of an adventure.

Breakfast Bread Pudding

$1/2$ loaf raisin bread
2 cups milk
3 eggs
dash nutmeg
$1/2$ teaspoon cinnamon
$1/2$ teaspoon vanilla
vanilla or lemon yogurt (optional)

Dice the bread and scatter it in a cold, buttered, heavy skillet. Whisk together the remaining ingredients, pour them over the bread, cover tightly, and cook over a low flame until the custard is set. Spoon into bowls and sauce with vanilla yogurt. Serves 4 to 6.

breakfast

Egg Mound Berry College

When we visited beautiful Berry College in the Georgia hills, this unusual egg dish was served. It's rich, eye-appealing, and ideal to make ahead of time. It keeps in the refrigerator for several days. For a quick breakfast on the go, serve it in individual disposable plastic drinking cups.

1 or 2 hard-boiled eggs per person
curry powder to taste
melted butter as needed for binding
sour cream or plain yogurt

Mash the eggs and combine with a drizzle of melted butter to make a smooth paste. Be conservative with the butter so you don't pile on too many calories and a greasy taste. Then add curry powder to taste. Spoon into individual serving containers of $\frac{1}{3}$ to $\frac{1}{2}$ cup each, and frost with sour cream. Chill. This is eaten cold, with a spoon.

Variation: This can also be served ice-cream style, in flat-bottom ice-cream cones. Fill, frost, and serve at once. Serve with a hot fruit compote, sweet rolls, and raspberry tea.

Hard-boiled eggs are the handiest of quick breakfasts. Keep a big supply on hand. Eat them cold, in casseroles, or add white sauce and a pinch of curry powder to make creamed eggs to serve over packaged rusk or Melba toast. To reduce fat, use a mixture that is half mashed eggs, half mashed tofu.

Fried Cornmeal Mush

Once a country breakfast staple, fried mush is rarely found on today's tables and more rarely still in restaurants. It's a penny-pincher food, and a boon to the RV cook because it can be made ahead of time. Make up several bricks of mush at home, refrigerate, then slice off as much as you need each day.

1 cup yellow cornmeal
$^1/_2$ cup cold water
1 teaspoon salt
3 cups boiling water
1 packet Butter Buds (optional)

Mix the cornmeal, salt, and cold water in a saucepan. Then, stirring constantly over a low flame, stir in the boiling water. Cover and cook over very low heat or in a double boiler, stirring occasionally, for 30 minutes. Stir in Butter Buds. Pour into an oiled 9-by-5-inch loaf pan and chill. Slice $^1/_2$ inch thick, dip in flour, and fry in butter until brown and crusty. Serve with syrup. Serves 4.

Variation: Before chilling, stir in a pound of bulk sausage that has been fried, drained, and crumbled.

Grits 'n' Eggs

This one-dish breakfast can be made in any quantity and with lots of variations. Regular grits are best, quick grits are second best, and instant grits are a distant third choice. This recipe comes from our friend Dick Langford, author of White Squall: The Last Voyage of Albatross. *Langford, the real-life English teacher on the doomed ship about which the movie "White Squall" was made, sometimes made this hearty breakfast for the boys on Sunday mornings.*

2 cups hot cooked grits, prepared according to package directions
3 to 4 eggs
3 to 4 tablespoons diced ham or crumbled precooked bacon or sausage
salt and pepper to taste
grated cheddar cheese (optional)

While grits are hot and bubbling, stir in eggs and meat. Keep stirring until eggs combine. Turn off heat, cover, and let stand until eggs are set. Season to taste and stir in grated cheese. Serves 2 (multiply as needed; any leftovers warm up well in the microwave).

With fruit or juice and hot coffee, this is a complete breakfast. For heartier appetites add toast, muffins, or biscuits.

breakfast

Bird's Nest Brunch

1 6-ounce box long-grain and wild rice mix
8 eggs
4 ounces Swiss cheese, grated
8 ounces precooked smoky sausage
$2/3$ cup evaporated milk
canned french fried onion rings

Preheat the oven to 350°F. Prepare rice mix according to package directions, spread in a buttered 9-by-13-inch pan or baking dish, and make 8 indentations with the back of a big spoon. Break an egg into each hollow. Slice sausage thinly and arrange around eggs, then smother with grated cheese. Pour milk over all. Sprinkle with french fried onion rings and bake just until heated through and eggs are set to your liking. Serves 4, with 2 eggs per person.

This goes well with streusel coffee cake.

Mexican Egg Casserole

6 corn tortillas
oil
1 small onion, chopped
1 clove garlic, mashed
2 tablespoons cooked, crumbled
  bacon
1 8-ounce can stewed
  tomatoes

1 10-ounce package frozen
  chopped spinach, thawed
  and drained
8 hard-boiled eggs, halved
1 8-ounce can or jar Mexican
  green sauce
4 ounces Monterey Jack
  cheese, grated

Sizzle tortillas in a little oil until crisp, then drain and cut into noodle-size strips. Scatter in the bottom of a greased 8-inch square pan. Saute onion and garlic in a little oil, then add bacon and tomatoes. Stir in spinach and spread mixture over the tortillas. Arrange the egg halves, yolk up, on this sauce. Pour green sauce over eggs, then sprinkle with grated cheese. Bake 15 minutes at 400°F. Serves 4 to 6.

This is a good choice to assemble ahead at home, keep refrigerated up to three days, and bake aboard. Baking time will be a few minutes longer

breakfast

if the casserole is chilled. If you want to add a bread course, stir up a boxed cornbread mix to bake with the casserole.

Breakfast Quiche

1 tube (8) refrigerated crescent rolls
8 ounces precooked, crumbled sausage (pork, turkey, or vegetarian)
8 ounces grated cheese
6 eggs
$1/2$ cup milk

Unroll crescent rolls and press to cover the bottom of a greased 9-by-13-inch baking pan. Bake 5 minutes at 375°F. Strew sausage and the grated cheese over the crust. Beat or shake eggs and milk together and pour over crust. Bake 30 to 35 minutes, or until set, at 350°F. Let stand 5 minutes before cutting into squares. Serves 4.

Apple-Topped Pancakes

your favorite pancakes
1 cup maple-flavored syrup
3 tablespoons raisins
dash cinnamon
1 15- to 18-ounce can pie-sliced apples (not apple pie filling)
vanilla yogurt

Heat syrup, raisins, and cinnamon with the undrained apples. Ladle over 4 big stacks of pancakes and top each with a dollop of vanilla yogurt. Serves 4.

Add crisp bacon strips and mugs of apple cinnamon tea.

Buy cooked, crumbled bacon, sold in supermarkets in cans, pouches, and jars. A little goes a long way in flavoring breakfast eggs or breads, and it's much better than imitation bacon bits.

Rediscover creamed chipped beef on toast. For a shortcut, serve it over Holland rusk.

Sun's Up Cheesecake

If you have one of these creamy cheesecakes in the refrigerator, you can get an early start on a hot summer day. To add fiber to the meal, serve bran muffins or a bowl of bran cereal. Although it will look more like a cheesecake if it's baked in a springform pan, it's easier to bake and carry in a deep-dish pie plate.

1 cup graham cracker crumbs
$^1/_2$ stick butter, melted
3 eggs
12 ounces cottage cheese
$^1/_2$ cup sugar
$^1/_4$ teaspoon salt
$^1/_4$ teaspoon cinnamon
$^1/_2$ teaspoon vanilla
16 ounces sour cream or yogurt
orange marmalade

Combine crumbs and butter and press into a pie plate or springform pan. Bake 10 minutes at 350°F. Whisk together all the other ingredients except the marmalade, pour onto the crust, and bake 30 minutes or until a knife inserted near the center comes out clean. Dot with orange marmalade, return to oven for 5 minutes more, then spread marmalade evenly. Cool, then chill. Serves 6.

Corned Beef Hashburgers

On a morning when you want to get an early start, serve these with crisp apples and cartons of juice for a complete drive-away breakfast you can eat with your hands, with no dishes to wash.

4 hamburger buns
butter
1 15-ounce can corned beef hash, chilled overnight
4 slices pineapple

Lightly butter the buns and fry them, butter side down, in a nonstick skillet until toasty. Set aside. Remove top and bottom of hash can, push out hash, and slice into 4 pieces. Fry slices in a lightly oiled nonstick skillet until crusty on both sides, topping each with a slice of pineapple for the last few minutes of cooking. Place each pineapple-hash stack in a hot bun. Serves 4.

A quicker version, although it isn't as good, is to put the sliced hash and pineapple into the unbuttered buns, wrap each individually, and microwave on High for 30 to 45 seconds each.

Breakfast Berries

Ah, the riches of RV travel! I'll never forget the raspberries we found during a trip to New Brunswick, the acres of wild blueberries in Ontario, the juicy sweetness of strawberries at a U-pick farm in Florida, and the wild blackberries, called brambles, we found during an RV trip through England.

1 stick butter, at room temperature	¹/₄ teaspoon salt
³/₄ cup rolled oats	¹/₄ teaspoon cinnamon
³/₄ cup brown sugar, firmly packed	4 cups berries
¹/₄ cup flour	¹/₄ cup white sugar
	1 tablespoon cornstarch
	2 tablespoons cold water

Using a pastry cutter, or two knives held scissors style, cut butter into flour, brown sugar, oats, salt, and cinnamon. Set aside. (This can be done the night before.) Put berries into a buttered 9-inch square pan, sprinkle with the white sugar, and drizzle with a mixture of the cornstarch and water. Pile lightly (don't pack it down) with the oats mixture and bake at 350°F about 40 minutes or until browned and bubbly. Serve warm in bowls with light cream, if you like. Serves 4.

Add buttery color and taste to pancake or waffle batter by adding a jar of baby food strained carrots or squash.

breakfast

Applesauce Muffins

2 cups biscuit mix
$1/4$ cup sugar
1 teaspoon apple pie spice
1 egg, beaten
2 tablespoons oil
8 ounces applesauce
$1/3$ cup milk

Topping
3 tablespoons butter, melted
$1/4$ cup sugar
$1/2$ teaspoon cinnamon

Combine biscuit mix with sugar and pie spice. Beat or shake together the egg, oil, applesauce, and milk. Combine wet and dry ingredients just until evenly mixed and spoon into 12 greased muffin cups. Bake about 12 minutes at 400°F, cool for a few minutes, remove from pan, and dip tops in the melted butter, then into a mixture of the sugar and cinnamon. Makes 12 muffins.

These go well with ham omelets.

Pineapple Dumplings

1 20-ounce can crushed pineapple, with juice
$1\,1/2$ cups orange juice
2 cups biscuit mix
$1/2$ teaspoon cinnamon
$1/3$ cup sugar
milk

Combine pineapple and its juice and the orange juice in a large skillet and bring to a boil. Add the sugar and cinnamon to the biscuit mix, then add enough milk to make a stiff dough, stirring only enough to moisten evenly. Drop by teaspoons atop the boiling fruit and keep at a simmer for 10 minutes, uncovered. Add more juice if needed. Cover, reduce heat, and simmer 10 minutes more. Serve at once, in bowls. Serves 4.

Rosy Fruit Coffee Cake

Because this is a coarse-textured cake, you don't have to use an electric mixer or beat it for hours by hand. Serve it in warm, fragrant squares alone with coffee, or with scrambled eggs.

1 can condensed tomato soup	$^1/_3$ cup chopped nuts
2 eggs	2 cups grated coconut
1 8-ounce can crushed pine-	$^1/_2$ stick butter
apple, with juice	$^1/_2$ cup flour
1 18-ounce package yellow	$^1/_3$ cup brown sugar, firmly
cake mix	packed
$^1/_3$ cup raisins	

Combine soup, eggs, and pineapple with its juice in a 9-by-13-inch pan and mix thoroughly. Stir in cake mix, raisins, nuts, and $1^1/_2$ cups of the coconut. Cut together the butter, brown sugar, flour, and remaining coconut, and sprinkle over the batter. Bake at 350°F for 45 to 50 minutes or until it tests done with a toothpick. Cut into 12 squares.

Variation: Try this with a spice cake mix.

Rainbow Dawn Dump Cake

As its name suggests, this dumps together and is baked and mixed right in the pan. It makes a moist, very sweet breakfast bread. When mixing, pay special attention to corners, where dry ingredients accumulate.

1 cup flour	splash vanilla
1 cup sugar	1 8-ounce can fruit cocktail,
$^1/_2$ teaspoon cinnamon	with juice
$^1/_2$ cup shredded bran cereal	applesauce, lemon yogurt, or
$^3/_4$ teaspoon baking soda	canned vanilla pudding
1 egg	

breakfast

Mix the dry ingredients in an 8-inch baking pan and mix in the egg, vanilla, and fruit cocktail and its juice. Bake 30 minutes at 350°F. Cut into 9 pieces, place in bowls, and top with vanilla pudding, applesauce, or lemon yogurt.

200-Mile Pancakes

These hearty, grainy pancakes are guaranteed to get you through the first 200 miles without the hungries, even though they contain no egg or fat. For an earlier getaway, mix up the dry ingredients the night before. Although it takes time to add all the different grains, they're the key to the rib-sticking richness of these flapjacks.

4 heaping tablespoons any combination oatmeal, cornmeal, oat bran, wheat bran, wheat germ

1 cup self-rising flour
$^1/_2$ teaspoon baking soda
1 $^1/_2$ cups buttermilk or sour milk

Combine the dry ingredients, then mix in milk just until everything is evenly moistened. Add a little more milk to make a thinner batter if you like. Spoon onto a hot greased or seasoned griddle and cook until browned on both sides. Serve with butter and syrup, sausage gravy, or fruit topping. Serves 2 to 3.

Breakfast Baba

Inspired by a classic dessert, baba au rhum, this is made the night before and served at room temperature for a quick breakfast.

1 plain (not herb flavored) 9-inch prepared pizza crust
1 cup sugar
1 cup strong tea
2 teaspoons rum flavoring
1 10-ounce can apricot pastry filling

breakfast

Pierce the pizza crust every inch or so with an ice pick and put in a cake or pie pan that it fits into with just a little room to spare. Boil sugar and tea 5 minutes, mix in rum flavoring, and pour slowly over the pizza shell. When it has soaked in, spread with apricot filling. Cover with plastic wrap and let stand overnight. Baba should be moist and sticky. Cut into 6 wedges and serve.

Hobo Breakfast

Wash and save tin cans to use in camping as disposable baking pans. For this recipe, you'll need one clean 12- to 16-ounce tin can per serving. Each is an all-in-one breakfast to eat on the go. Once baked, they'll keep several days in the refrigerator, so you can grab them as needed.

frozen bread dough
hard-boiled eggs
real bacon bits
squeeze margarine

Grease tin cans using a nonstick spray. Cut the frozen dough into 1-inch-thick slices. Press a slice of dough in the bottom of each can, sprinkle lightly with bacon bits, top with a peeled hard-boiled egg, sprinkle with a little more bacon, and top with another chunk of dough, pressing it firmly over the egg. Drizzle with margarine. The can should be only half full.

Let rise just until the dough reaches the top of the can (it will rise more as it bakes, so don't place it too close to the top of the oven), then bake at 350°F until the dough is golden brown. Let cool slightly. If bread doesn't lift easily out of the can, remove the can bottom with a can opener and push through. Serve in a paper napkin. Eat warm or cold, plain or with butter and jam.

Substitute paper-thin slices of smoked salmon for the Canadian bacon when making eggs Benedict. Make Hollandaise sauce from a package mix.

Spoon canned tapioca pudding into serving dishes, top with well-drained peach slices, and sprinkle with All-Bran or wheat germ for a sweet breakfast with texture contrast.

Fanciful French Toast

bread
mincemeat from a jar
eggs
milk
rum (optional)
butter for frying
syrup or powdered sugar

Spread mincemeat on the bread to make 1 or 2 "sandwiches" per person. Whisk together eggs and milk, and a splash of rum if you like. Dip sandwiches in the mixture; coat well but do not soak. Fry sandwiches in butter until brown and toasty on each side. Serve with maple syrup or sprinkle with powdered sugar.

Variations: Make the sandwiches with your favorite jam, peanut butter and jelly, peanut butter and real bacon bits, or mashed bananas. Turned into French toast, the sandwiches take on new heartiness, taste, and aroma.

For savory treats, make the sandwiches with cheese, egg salad, or bacon and tomato. Complement the flavors with white sauce, dill sauce, Hollandaise, or a tangy tomato salsa.

Open-Face Sun-Up Sandwiches

6 thick slices hearty bread, buttered
3 ounces cream cheese, at room temperature
cinnamon sugar
6 teaspoons real bacon bits
6 pear halves (fresh or canned), sliced
6 thin slices Swiss or Jarlsberg cheese

Arrange bread, butter side down, on a lightly greased baking sheet. Spread thinly with cream cheese and sprinkle very lightly with cinnamon sugar. Sprinkle with bacon bits, then cover with a layer of pears. Bake 5 minutes at 350°F, place a slice of cheese on each, and return to oven until bread is toasty on the bottom and the cheese has melted over the pears. Makes 6 sandwiches (hearty eaters may need more than one!).

Haystacks

$^1/_2$ cup crushed shredded wheat or other cereal
3 tablespoons butter, melted
4 tablespoons brown sugar
3 tablespoons chopped nuts
3 tablespoons flaked coconut
dash cinnamon
6 peach or pear halves

Mix all ingredients except the fruit. Arrange the drained fruit, cut side up, in a buttered casserole or individual ramekins and fill centers with "haystacks" of the wheat mixture. Bake at 425°F until the top is lightly browned and the fruit is well heated. Serves 6 as a breakfast fruit or 3 as a breakfast main dish.

Upset Applecart

$^1/_2$ stick butter
8 ounces applesauce
$^1/_4$ cup raisins
$^1/_4$ cup chopped nuts
$^1/_4$ cup brown sugar, firmly packed
$^1/_2$ teaspoon apple pie spice
1 tube (10) refrigerated biscuits

breakfast

Melt butter in a deep-dish pie pan in a 425°F oven, turning pan so it is well coated. Stir in remaining ingredients except biscuits and return to oven for 3 to 5 minutes. Top the hot mixture with the biscuits and return to oven for 15 minutes or until the biscuits are golden brown. Working carefully and wearing thick oven mitts (the apple mixture will be boiling hot), place a serving plate over the pie dish and flip over. Serve at once as a breakfast main course, or as a coffee cake with a ham omelet. Serves 5, with 2 biscuits per person.

To double this recipe, use a 9-by-13-inch pan, but don't attempt to flip it. Serve it with a spoon, sauce side up.

New Orleans Breakfast Puffs (Calas)

Make the dough the night before. On a morning when you have time to fuss a bit, fry these puffs to golden perfection while sending out a scent that will bring the crew out of their bedrolls in a hurry. This is an ideal way to use leftover rice.

2 cups cooked rice	1 teaspoon vanilla
2 cups biscuit mix	oil for deep frying
2 tablespoons sugar	
1 $^1/_2$ teaspoons apple pie	*Glaze*
spice	1 cup powdered sugar
2 eggs	$^1/_2$ teaspoon vanilla
$^1/_2$ cup milk	1 to 2 tablespoons water

Combine dry ingredients in a roomy bowl. Whisk or shake together wet ingredients and stir into dry ingredients just until well moistened. Cover and refrigerate overnight. Heat about 2 inches of oil in a roomy, deep skillet to 400°F. Calas will be soggy if the fat is not hot enough; as a test, drop in a small cube of white bread, which should brown in 50 seconds. Drop cold batter by tablespoons into hot oil and brown them on one side, then turn and brown the other. While calas are cooking, combine the glaze ingredients. Remove the hot calas to a bowl lined with paper towels and drizzle with glaze. Serves 6.

Spoon nonfat vanilla yogurt into serving dishes, top with well-drained peach slices, and sprinkle with granola, fine-tuning amounts for individual tastes, for a quick breakfast on the go.

breakfast

Cajun Huevos Rancheros (Mexican Eggs with a Creole Accent)

Here is another only-in-America blend of ethnic flavors. It's a one-dish wonder and easy as pie, especially when you make the grits mixture ahead of time at home. It will keep for four to five days in the RV refrigerator.

4 cups hot cooked grits	seasoned flour or breadcrumbs
8 ounces smoked sausage, diced	fried or poached eggs
2 tablespoons grated cheese	Creole tomato sauce
2 tablespoons butter	grated jack cheese (optional)

Stir sausage, 2 tablespoons cheese, and butter into grits and spread in a buttered jellyroll pan. Cover with waxed paper and chill overnight. Cut into 12 squares. Stack the squares, separated by waxed paper, in plastic bags and store them in the refrigerator. To assemble the dish, dip each square of the cold grits in seasoned flour or breadcrumbs and fry in butter until brown and toasty. Top each with a fried or poached egg and hot Creole tomato sauce—your own favorite recipe or one from a can or jar. Sprinkle on some grated jack cheese for added richness. Serves 12.

Stuffed Ham Omelet

1 1/2 cups cold stuffing
4 slices square deli-baked ham
2 tablespoons butter
8 eggs
1/2 cup milk

Use leftover stuffing or add hot water to a mix to make $1\frac{1}{2}$ cups. Form stuffing into 4 sausage-shaped cylinders and roll up each one in a slice of ham. Melt butter in a 10-inch nonstick skillet. Add ham rolls, seam side down, in 4 "spokes." Whisk together eggs and milk, pour over ham, cover, and cook over medium heat until eggs are just set. Uncover and let stand 5 minutes. Using a utensil safe for nonstick coatings, cut omelet into 4 portions with a ham roll in the center of each and place on plates.

breakfast

Five

Bread: A Lust for Loafing

As You Like It Loaf

This versatile loaf can be made with many variations. Use what you have on hand, including lots of imagination and daring.

3 cups flour (can include up to $1/2$ cup whole wheat flour, cornmeal, or oatmeal)
2 teaspoons baking powder
$1/2$ teaspoon baking soda
$1/2$ teaspoon salt
1 teaspoon apple pie spice
1 egg
$1/4$ cup oil
$1/2$ cup light molasses, corn syrup, or maple syrup
$3/4$ cup buttermilk, sour milk, or yogurt thinned with a little milk

Add-Ins
1 cup grated carrots, pineapple, or apples
1 cup mashed pumpkin, bananas, or sweet potatoes
1 cup fresh blueberries, raspberries, or strawberries
$1/2$ cup finely chopped cranberries
$1/2$ cup raisins (optional)
$1/2$ cup chopped nuts (optional)

Grease a 9-by-5-inch loaf pan. Mix dry ingredients in a large bowl and make a well in the center. Whisk together the egg, sweetener, oil, and milk and add all at once to dry ingredients. Mix just until everything is evenly moistened. Quickly fold in your choice of one of the add-ins, and the nuts and raisins (if desired). Pour batter into pan and bake at 350°F for about 60 minutes or until bread tests done with a toothpick. Let stand 15 minutes in the pan, then turn out onto a rack. Cool, then slice with a serrated knife. Makes 1 loaf.

This is delicious hot but will slice better if wrapped and stored overnight.

Easy Cheesy Danish

1 package (about 12) brown-and-serve rolls
8 ounces cream cheese, at room temperature
2 eggs
$^1/_2$ cup sugar
1 tablespoon lemon juice
1 teaspoon vanilla

Heat oven to 400°F. Grease a pan just large enough to fit the block of rolls. Place rolls, packed tightly together, in pan and, using the handle of a wooden spoon, poke 3 or 4 holes in each roll almost all the way to the bottom. Beat other ingredients together and carefully pour into the holes in the rolls. Bake just until rolls are golden and the cheese mixture has set, about 8 to 12 minutes. Makes 12 rolls.

Shop for canned breads to have on hand for emergencies and unexpected guests. In supermarkets and gourmet stores you'll find canned corn tortillas, Boston brown bread, canned date and nut bread, and perhaps other specialty breads. However, avoid tinned "export" biscuits, which may not be actually "canned." The tin provides protection against breakage but the crackers will spoil just as if they were in a regular package.

> Quick breads cut easiest if they have been tightly wrapped and "seasoned" overnight. However, they are hard to resist when fresh and hot. A serrated bread knife will do the best cutting job.

Microwave Health Bread

Throw this together in seconds and bake it in mere minutes. It can be baked in any suitable microwave-safe container, such as a bakeproof measuring cup or a wide-mouth, pint-size canning jar. The bread will be firmer and easier to slice if you cool it first.

1 cup whole wheat flour
$1/2$ cup cornmeal
1 teaspoon baking soda
1 cup buttermilk, sour milk, or thin yogurt
$1/3$ cup molasses
$1/2$ cup raisins
$1/2$ cup chopped nuts

Combine dry ingredients except raisins and nuts. Add wet ingredients. Stir just until evenly moistened, then fold in raisins and nuts. Pour half the batter into a greased 1-pint (2-cup), microwave-safe container, cover loosely with waxed paper or microwave-safe wrap, and microwave on Medium 5 to 7 minutes, rotating every few minutes, until firm around the edges. Let stand 5 minutes before turning out. Repeat with other half of batter. Slice and serve with a fancy butter. Makes 2 pint-size loaves.

This is a very dense, moist bread, not suitable for sandwiches.

bread

The Best Bran Muffins

This recipe calls for bran, not an expensive bran cereal. If your super-market doesn't sell plain bran, find it at health-food stores. Molasses gives a dark, tangy taste but you can also use honey or maple syrup.

2 cups flour	$^1/_2$ cup molasses
1 $^1/_2$ cups wheat or oat bran	$^1/_4$ cup oil
$^1/_2$ teaspoon salt	$^1/_2$ cup raisins
1 $^1/_2$ teaspoons baking soda	1 tablespoon fresh orange
2 cups buttermilk or yogurt	zest or 1 teaspoon orange
thinned with milk	or lemon extract

Mix all dry ingredients (the night before, if you like). Dump in liquids, mix just to moisten evenly, and fold in raisins. Fill 24 greased muffin cups $^2/_3$ full and bake 15 to 20 minutes at 425°F. Makes 24 muffins.

Butterscotch Pecan Rolls

1 package (12) brown-and-serve rolls
1 4-serving package butterscotch pudding mix (not instant)
6 ounces pecan pieces

Line 12 muffin cups with cupcake papers, place a roll in each, and bake according to manufacturer's directions. Meanwhile, prepare the pudding mix according to package directions and fold in pecans. Using an ice pick or the handle of a wooden spoon, puncture the hot rolls several times at varying depths and pour in the hot pudding. Cool for a few minutes, then move to serving plates. Gooey and good! Makes 12 rolls.

bread

Spicy Carrot Loaf

2 $1/4$ cups flour
1 $1/3$ cups instant oats
$3/4$ cup dark brown sugar,
    firmly packed
$1/2$ cup raisins
4 teaspoons baking powder
$1/2$ teaspoon baking soda
dash salt

1 teaspoon apple pie spice
$1/3$ cup salad oil
$3/4$ cup water
2 eggs
2 3- to 4-ounce jars baby
    food strained carrots

Combine dry ingredients and mix well. Combine wet ingredients. Add wet ingredients to dry and mix only until evenly moistened. Spread in a greased 9-by-5-inch loaf pan and bake at 350°F for 70 to 75 minutes. Test for doneness. Let stand 10 to 15 minutes, then turn out. Makes 1 loaf.

Quick Cinnammmmmuffins

2 sticks butter, at room temperature
8 ounces regular or low-fat sour cream
2 cups self-rising flour
cinnamon sugar

Whisk together butter and sour cream and stir in self-rising flour just until blended. Sprinkle with cinnamon sugar. Fill 12 paper-lined muffin cups $2/3$ full and bake 25 to 30 minutes at 350°F. Makes 12 muffins.

These are so rich and buttery, they don't really need additional butter. Serve them plain or with strawberry jam.

bread

Tin Can Breads

Carefully remove the tops of 12- to 16-ounce fruit and vegetable tins, leaving clean rims. Rinse and dry the tins and save four or five to make this recipe on the road. You'll have no loaf pans to wash.

2 cups sugar
2 teaspoons salt
4 cups flour
1 tablespoon apple pie spice
1 tablespoon baking powder
$^1/_2$ teaspoon baking soda
4 eggs

1 cup oil
2 cups mashed pumpkin or bananas
$^2/_3$ cup milk
$^1/_2$ cup raisins and/or $^1/_2$ cup broken nuts (optional)

Combine the dry ingredients in a plastic bag and shake to mix. In a roomy bowl whisk together wet ingredients, then add dry ingredients all at once. Mix only to moisten evenly, then fold in the nuts and raisins, if you like. Fill 4 or 5 greased tin cans half full and bake at 350°F until the loaves test done (a toothpick plunged into the center will come out clean). Let cool completely, wrap, and refrigerate any you won't use within a day or two. Makes 4 or 5 can-size loaves.

To serve, remove can bottoms with a can opener and push out the bread. Slice into rounds. This bread toasts deliciously in a skillet: butter slices lightly and fry them in a nonstick frying pan until they are brown and crusty.

South in Yo' Mouth Biscuits

The secret to making real buttermilk biscuits Southern style is to use all-vegetable white shortening and the soft wheat flour sold in the South under such brand names as Martha White and White Lily. Buttermilk is best, but you can substitute a cup of sweet milk soured with a splash of lemon juice or vinegar.

2 cups self-rising flour, Southern regional brand
pinch baking soda
1 tablespoon sugar
¾ cup shortening*
1 cup buttermilk

Mix dry ingredients and cut in shortening with a pastry blender or two knives until mixture is filled with lumps about the size of peas. Stir in buttermilk and turn out dough onto well-floured paper towels. Knead lightly 4 to 5 times (do not overknead) and pat into a circle. Cut into rounds and bake 10 to 12 minutes at 425°F. Serve hot. Makes about 12 biscuits (depending on the size of your biscuit cutter).

*To measure shortening, add ¼ cup water to a 1-cup measure and add shortening until water comes to the top. Pour off the water. You now have ¾ cup shortening.

Your Own Breadsticks

day-old hot-dog buns
1 stick butter
poppy seeds, toasted sesame seeds, or grated hard cheese

Pull apart bun halves and cut each half into 3 strips. Dip each lightly in melted butter, and then in seeds or cheese. Bake on a cookie sheet at 350°F about 15 minutes or until golden. Each bun makes 6 breadsticks.

Corny Bread

½ stick butter
3 cups biscuit mix
2 eggs
16 ounces sour cream
1 15- or 16-ounce can cream style corn
8 ounces cheddar cheese, grated
½ teaspoon paprika

Melt butter in a 9-by-13-inch pan and tilt to coat pan well. Put biscuit mix in a large bowl. Whisk together eggs, sour cream, cheese, corn, and paprika, and mix with the biscuit mix just until everything is well moistened. Bake at 425°F about 30 minutes or until lightly browned around the edges and springy in the middle. Cut into 18 squares.

Variation: Add 2 cups sautéed onions, drained and cooled, to the corn mixture.

Master Scone Recipe

To make your own scone mix, multiply the dry ingredients as many times as you wish. Keep tightly covered in a cool place. When ready to use, just add the wet ingredients as listed below.

2 cups flour
2 tablespoons sugar
2 teaspoons baking powder
$1/2$ teaspoon baking soda
pinch salt
$1/4$ cup cold butter
$2/3$ cup buttermilk or sour milk
1 egg

Combine dry ingredients. Cut butter into pieces and then cut it into dry ingredients with two knives or a pastry blender. (British cooks do it with their fingers, using a quick, light, pinching motion.) Beat egg and milk together and mix in quickly. Knead on a floured paper towel 5 to 6 times, just to mix well (unlike yeast breads, which improve with kneading, quick breads need a light touch). Pat ball of dough into an 8-inch circle on a greased baking sheet and score it into 8 wedges (do not cut through). Bake about 15 minutes at 425°F, or until golden. Cut into 8 wedges and serve warm with butter and jam.

Variations:

◆ For a Scottish touch, substitute brown sugar for white, and substitute $1/4$ cup rolled oats for $1/4$ cup flour. Sprinkle with another $1/4$ cup oats before scoring dough.

♦ Additions to mix in after cutting in butter:
  ♦ for a Mexican touch, add $\frac{1}{2}$ cup Mexicorn
  ♦ add $\frac{1}{2}$ cup freshly grated cheese, then serve hot cheese scones with green salad vinaigrette for lunch
  ♦ for fruity breakfast scones, add $\frac{1}{2}$ cup cut-up dried prunes or apricots and $\frac{1}{4}$ cup chopped walnuts
  ♦ to accompany a scrambled eggs breakfast, add 2 tablespoons real bacon bits

Yeast Bread

Some RV travelers don't take the time to bake yeast bread, while others wouldn't leave home without their bread machines. There is no real substitute for yeast bread, so keep a box of hot roll mix, a tube of refrigerated bread dough, or a loaf or two of frozen bread dough on hand, to be raised and baked when needed. Here's a quick compromise that reduces the time and steps needed to make a yeast loaf from scratch. It needs little kneading. Note that it calls for self-rising flour, which makes it twice as fast and twice as foolproof.

1 package yeast	$\frac{1}{4}$ cup sugar
1 stick butter, melted in $\frac{1}{2}$ cup warm water and $1\frac{1}{2}$ cups warm (not hot) milk	2 eggs, beaten
	6 to 7 cups self-rising flour

In a large bowl, sprinkle yeast over warm butter-liquid mixture to dissolve it, then stir in remaining ingredients, adding enough flour to make a stiff dough. Cover bowl with a clean towel and place in a warm place, away from any wind, until dough doubles in bulk. Turn out onto a clean, floured dishtowel or board and knead in more flour as necessary to make dough easy to handle. Divide in half, shape into 2 loaves, place in greased 9-by-5-inch loaf pans, and let rise until double in bulk. Bake at 400°F until loaves are golden brown and sound hollow when tapped. Makes 2 loaves.

bread

> To make your own economical biscuit mix, cut 4 cups regular or butter-flavored shortening into 16 cups self-rising flour. Keep tightly lidded in a cool place.

Focaccia Buon Appetito

Focaccia is bread dough baked in a large, flat sheet. It can be served on its own, topped to make snacks or a meal, or used for sandwiches. Refrigerated dough is less authentic but easier to handle.

1 tube refrigerated pizza or breadstick dough
2 tablespoons virgin olive oil
grated Parmesan cheese

Spray a cookie sheet and press out dough as thin as possible, using your fingers and leaving finger-size "dimples" in the surface. Drizzle with olive oil and sprinkle lightly with Parmesan cheese. Bake at 400°F until golden. Cut into 12 squares and serve.

Try serving this as a bread course with saucers of olive oil and balsamic vinegar for dipping.

Variations:

◆ Before baking, sprinkle with dried or fresh herbs, such as basil, oregano, or parsley.

◆ Cut into squares and use to make conventional or open-face sandwiches.

◆ Cut into bite-size pieces to use as a base for canapés.

◆ Brush baked squares with olive oil, dot with bits of plum tomato, sprinkle with a little basil, and top with more cheese. Serve for lunch or as a snack.

◆ Cut into cubes and add to a salad just before tossing.

Porridge Muffins

When you have just a little oatmeal left over from breakfast, make these hearty muffins to go with soup or stew for lunch or dinner.

1²/3 cups flour	1½ cups milk
2 tablespoons brown sugar	1 cup cooked oatmeal
2 teaspoons baking powder	2 eggs
dash salt	1 tablespoon olive oil

Combine dry ingredients in a bowl. Beat together wet ingredients, pour into the dry ingredients, and mix just until everything is moistened evenly. Fill 12 paper-lined or well-greased muffin cups ²/3 full and bake at 425°F for about 20 to 25 minutes. Let stand a few minutes before turning out of the pan. Makes 12 muffins.

Gingerbread

Think of this gingerbread as a bread, not a dessert. It's a zesty companion for a meal of baked ham and scalloped potatoes, or bratwurst with boiled and buttered potatoes.

2¼ cups flour
1 teaspoon ground ginger
1 teaspoon baking soda
1 cup beer
½ cup oil
½ cup light molasses (not blackstrap)
1 egg, beaten

Stir together the dry ingredients in a bowl, then whisk together the wet ingredients and dump all at once into the dry. Mix just to moisten evenly and turn into a greased 9-inch square pan. Bake 45 to 50 minutes at 325°F. Let cool 10 minutes before cutting into 9 squares.

bread

For easier mixing of the wet ingredients for a quick bread, shake them up in a tightly lidded container (such as a juice bottle) that you're about to throw away, and you won't have to wash a bowl and beater.

Bran Muffins Jarlsberg

When we want to hit the road very early, I assemble these ingredients the night before, bake the muffins while we're getting ready to roll, then serve them on the go with hot coffee. They are rich and moist enough to be eaten plain, without butter, and are hearty enough to constitute a real stick-to-the-ribs breakfast.

1/2 stick butter, softened
1/2 cup flour
1/3 cup brown sugar, firmly packed
1/4 cup miller's bran
1/4 cup chopped nuts
1 16-ounce package date bread mix

1 cup milk
1/3 cup dried cranberries
1/4 cup oil
1 egg
3/4 cup grated Jarlsberg cheese

In a small bowl mix butter, flour, and sugar until crumbly. Set aside. In a large bowl combine remaining ingredients. Mix with a wooden spoon just until well blended with no dry particles. Fill 12 paper-lined muffin cups 2/3 full, and sprinkle with crumb mixture. Bake at 400°F for about 20 minutes or until they test done. Cool in the pan 5 minutes, then remove to cooking rack. Serve warm-m-m-m. Makes 12 muffins.

Beer Bread

Some may find the taste and smell of beer distasteful, but I urge everyone to discover the convenience and springy texture of beer bread. The alcohol cooks away, leaving a yeasty taste and breadlike consistency that slices, toasts, and makes sandwiches better than any other quick bread.

bread

The recipe for beer bread has been printed time and again, so it hardly needs repeating here except as a starting point for the variations I have developed.

1 12-ounce bottle or can beer (can be nonalcoholic)
3 cups self-rising flour
1 tablespoon sugar

Pour the (room temperature) beer into a medium bowl, add the flour and sugar, and blend only until it is evenly moistened. Turn into a greased 9-by-5-inch loaf pan or 1-quart deep casserole and bake at 350°F for about 45 minutes or until it's brown and sounds hollow when tapped. Makes 1 loaf.

Use a serrated bread knife to slice this bread. Like most breads, beer bread tastes best when it is hot but will be easier to slice thinly and evenly for toast or sandwiches if it has been cooled, wrapped, and "seasoned" overnight.

Variations:

◆ Substitute up to 1 cup whole wheat, rye, soy, or oat flour for 1 cup of the self-rising flour. Always add 1 teaspoon baking powder and an extra pinch of salt per cup of non-self-rising flour.

◆ When using part rye flour, add 1 teaspoon of fresh orange zest and 1 tablespoon of caraway seeds to the batter.

◆ Substitute honey, molasses, or maple syrup for the sugar. To intensify maple flavor, add a few drops of maple extract.

◆ To make a fruit and nut loaf, add up to 1 cup of cut-up dried apricots, dates, candied cherries, raisins, chopped walnuts, pitted prunes, or the like.

◆ To make raisin bread, add 1 teaspoon cinnamon and an extra tablespoon of sugar, plus 1 cup raisins to the batter.

◆ Invent an herb-cheese bread by adding 1 teaspoon of your favorite dried herbs and 2 to 3 teaspoons grated hard cheese.

bread

Six

Soup's On

Soup is the essence of cold-weather comfort cuisine, one of life's most intoxicating pleasures. Make a simple soup into a hearty meal by adding a salad and mountains of hot bread. Have soup for lunch, for a snack, for a calmer at bedtime, and as a soothing healer for road-jangled nerves.

Most of these are shortcut soups, yet they have superb flavor and a touch of class.

Comforting Winter Soups

Corn Chowder with Brie

1 6-ounce round of Brie
dried dill weed
1 small onion, minced
2 tablespoons butter
1 15- or 16-ounce can cream-style corn
1 12- to 16-ounce can chicken broth
1 can evaporated skim milk

Cut Brie into 8 wedges and place 2 each in 4 soup bowls. Sprinkle lightly with dill weed and let come to room temperature. Sauté onion in butter until tender, add corn and chicken broth, and boil for about 2 minutes. Remove from heat, add milk and more dill weed (to taste), and ladle immediately over Brie. Serves 4.

Serve with pilot crackers, sweet butter, and a fruity dessert such as blueberry buckle or apple betty.

Seafood Bisque

1 can condensed cream of mushroom soup
1 can condensed tomato soup
1 soup-can water
1 13-ounce can evaporated milk
1 6-ounce can shrimp or crab, drained and picked over
sherry

Combine soups, water, and milk in a saucepan and stir over medium flame until smooth and well heated. Do not boil. Stir in seafood and continue heating. Ladle into bowls and add a splash of sherry to each. Serves 4.

Golden Potato Soup

2 servings instant mashed potatoes
1 4-ounce jar baby food strained carrots
1 tablespoon instant onion flakes
1 can condensed chicken broth
1 soup-can milk
salt and pepper to taste
fresh parsley

Prepare potatoes according to package directions. Stir in remaining ingredients and heat, stirring often, until thoroughly heated. Sprinkle with chopped parsley, if you like. Serves 4 as an appetizer or 2 as a main dish.

soup

Poached Egg Soup

This makes a light supper or a quick roadside lunch.

1 14-ounce can chicken broth
$^1/_4$ cup water
2 eggs
1 cup shredded lettuce
grated Parmesan or Romano cheese

Bring broth and water to a boil in a skillet and, using a spoon to make a whirlpool in the center, poach eggs one at a time. When each egg is done, remove it to a soup bowl. Add lettuce to broth and cook just until wilted. Spoon broth over eggs, sprinkle with cheese, and serve with buttered rusks. Serves 2.

Chunky Chicken Clam Chowder

1 can condensed cream of chicken soup
1 soup-can milk
1 10-ounce package frozen mixed vegetables
pinch dried thyme
2 5- or 6-ounce cans chunk chicken
1 6-ounce can clams, with juice
butter

soup

Mix everything but butter in a roomy saucepan and simmer over low heat until vegetables are done. Before serving, put a pat of butter in each soup bowl. Serves 4.

Serve with oyster crackers or big, buttery, homemade croutons.

Toasted bread with broiled cheese on top can be used as a hearty, meal-making topping on almost any hot soup, not just French onion. Float it atop bowls of minestrone, cream of potato, or cream of asparagus.

Pleasant Peasant Ragout

This is a very filling soup/stew to serve on a cold night. It is a good choice for preparing at home, to be warmed up in the RV's microwave.

6 meaty, skinless chicken thighs
6 sweet Italian sausages
2 tablespoons oil
1 large onion, diced
2 cloves garlic, mashed
1 16-ounce can tomatoes
1 teaspoon mixed Italian herbs

1 green pepper, diced
2 15- or 16-ounce cans white
   kidney beans
1 can condensed beef broth
1 soup-can water, mixed with
   red wine

Brown chicken and sausage in hot oil in a roomy saucepan. Continue stirring and frying while sautéing onion and garlic. Pour off excess fat. Add tomatoes, broth, wine, and herbs. Cover and simmer 15 to 20 minutes over low heat. Add beans and green pepper, cover, and simmer 10 minutes more. Place a piece of chicken and a sausage in each bowl. Divide broth among the portions. Serves 6.

Add a leafy salad and canned Boston brown bread spread with whipped cream cheese. Give everyone a licorice whip to eat while you all wind up the evening with a brisk twilight hike.

Rosy Glow Soup

1 can condensed cream of mushroom soup
2 3- to 4-ounce jars baby food strained beets
1 soup-can milk
sour cream (optional)

Whisk together soup, milk, and beets and heat thoroughly. Add a dollop of sour cream to each bowl, if you like. Serves 2.

Variations: Stir in baby food strained carrots, squash, or peas to create other cream soups. Add a dash of nutmeg or a dash of dried dill weed.

soup

When making vegetable soup that calls for rice or pasta, use a medley of barley, rice, orzo, millet, broken spaghetti, and what have you, rather than just one starch.

Hurry-Up Thuringer and Bean Soup

This robust soup gets off to a fast start because you begin with fully cooked meat and beans.

6 ounces precooked smoked Thuringer sausage links
1 16-ounce can great northern beans, undrained and mashed with a fork
1 small onion, diced
1 tablespoon minced garlic
1 cup beef broth
$1/4$ cup dry sherry
$3/4$ teaspoon cumin
green onion, chives, parsley (optional)

Slice sausage and set aside. Combine beans, onion, garlic, broth, sherry, and cumin in a 2-quart microware dish. Cover and vent, and cook on High 5 minutes, stirring every minute, until thoroughly hot. Add sausage and cook another minute or so to heat through. Garnish with onion, parsley, and chives, if you like. Serves 2 to 3.

This hearty, warming soup calls for slabs of bread torn from a fresh French loaf, an apple salad, and tin roof sundaes for dessert.

Lightning Chowder

1 can condensed cream of celery soup
1 can condensed cream of potato soup
2 soup-cans milk or cream
1 7-ounce can or pouch tuna
4 pats butter
dried thyme

Whisk together soups and milk in a saucepan and stir in tuna. Heat until steaming. Place a pat of butter in each soup bowl, sprinkle lightly with thyme, and ladle soup over all. Serves 4.

Mock Turtle Soup

Because this is such a thick and meaty soup, it makes a perfect main course when served with a salad and rolls. Its secret is a classic roux made with real butter and cooked to coppery perfection. It rewarms well in the microwave or in a double boiler, so it can be made at home and reheated on the first or second night out.

1 tablespoon oil	4 cups water
1 tablespoon butter	4 beef bouillon cubes
1 1/2 pounds ground turkey	
1 large onion, diced	*Roux*
2 ribs celery, diced	2 sticks butter
3 cloves garlic, minced	3/4 cup flour
1 tablespoon cumin	
1 tablespoon thyme	*Garnish*
1 tablespoon oregano	sherry
3 bay leaves,	3 to 4 hard-boiled eggs,
1 15- or 16-ounce can	chopped
pureed tomatoes	

In a roomy skillet or pot melt 1 tablespoon of butter with oil and brown turkey with onion, celery, and garlic until vegetables are just tender. Stir in spices, bay leaves, tomatoes, water, and bouillon cubes and simmer, uncovered, about 45 minutes over very low flame. Stir occasionally.

Meanwhile, make the roux. In a heavy skillet melt butter, then stir in flour. Cook, stirring continuously, over a medium flame for 20 to 25 minutes or until mixture is a dark-copper color.

Remove bay leaves from soup, stir in roux, and cook, stirring, over medium heat until thick and hot. Ladle into soup bowls, sprinkle with chopped hard-boiled eggs and pass sherry in a cruet or a shaker-top bottle (e.g., a soy sauce bottle). Serves 6 to 8.

soup

Summer Soups to Serve Cold

Cold Bean-Tomato Soup

Make this ahead of time at home and chill for up to two days while flavors mingle and marry. Somewhat like gazpacho, this is hearty enough to serve as a main dish in hot weather.

1 16-ounce can diced tomatoes, with juice
1 16-ounce can tomato juice
1 19-ounce can white beans, drained
1 small green pepper, minced
2 tablespoons olive oil
1 tablespoon lime juice
1 small Bermuda onion, diced
1/4 teaspoon garlic salt
1/4 teaspoon onion salt
dash Tabasco
minced fresh parsley

Place everything except parsley in a bowl, cover, and chill thoroughly. Ladle into bowls and shower with minced parsley. Serves 3 to 4.

Cucumber Soup

2 medium cucumbers, peeled, seeded, and finely chopped (about 2 cups)
2 quarts (8 cups) buttermilk
1 teaspoon dried dill weed
1 tablespoon dried chopped chives
salt and pepper to taste
1/4 cup chopped fresh parsley

Mix all ingredients, adjust seasonings, and chill thoroughly. (If you have fresh dill, use it generously instead of dried.) If you don't have fresh parsley, use none. Serves 6 to 8.

soup

Orange Soup

5 cups tomato juice or
   tomato juice cocktail
$1/2$ cup orange juice con-
   centrate, undiluted
2 tablespoons lemon juice

2 tablespoons sugar
salt, pepper, garlic salt to taste
thin slices lemon
lemon yogurt (optional)

Mix all ingredients together and chill. Garnish each serving with a slice of lemon and a dollop of lemon yogurt. Makes $5^{1}/_2$ cups.

Avocado Soup

3 medium avocados, mashed to a smooth paste
2 tablespoons lemon juice
2 cups plain nonfat yogurt
2 cups broth (beef, vegetable, or chicken)
dash paprika
onion salt to taste

Mix avocados with lemon juice, then gradually stir in remaining ingredients. Chill. Serves 4 to 6.

Jellied Elegance Soup

2 cans jellied consommé, chilled
2 tablespoons lemon juice
1 2-ounce jar caviar
1 small onion, minced
sour cream

Slice each roll of consommé into 4 serving-size rounds. Mix caviar with lemon juice and scatter on consommé. Sprinkle with minced onion and top with a dab of sour cream. Serve as a salad; it is eaten with a fork. Serves 8.

soup

Fast Lane

◆ Save an empty soy sauce bottle (the kind with a plastic shaker insert), and fill with sherry. Pass at the table to splash into soups, chili, and stews.

◆ To turn a thin soup into a hearty main dish, add milk to biscuit mix to make a thick dough and drop by teaspoons into boiling soup. Boil 10 minutes uncovered, 10 minutes more tightly covered without peeking. A ½ cup of biscuit mix makes enough dumplings for 3 to 4 cups soup.

◆ To enrich a thin soup, beat a couple of eggs well and pour them in a thin stream into the boiling soup while stirring in a swirl. Eggs will cook in long, noodlelike strings.

◆ When you're out of evaporated milk for use in chowder, mix up a batch of double-strength nonfat powdered milk. Add an extra pat of butter.

◆ To make canned soups taste more like homemade, combine two or more flavors. Good combinations include cream of tomato with split pea, minestrone with bean, cream of potato with New England clam chowder, or cream of mushroom with broccoli cheese.

◆ Make your favorite oyster stew recipe using bay scallops instead and discover a new taste treat.

◆ To thicken any soup, stir in 1 to 2 tablespoons rolled oats or potato flakes.

soup

Seven

Anytime Foods: Sandwiches, Appetizers, Snacks

This is my collection of recipes for times when you need a nosh, a quick lunch, or a company snack.

Of all the foods we rely on in the gadabout life, cheese sandwiches lead the way. They can be crammed into a fanny pack for a day hike, snuck into a movie or ball game, or nibbled while stuck in traffic or waiting in a ferry line.

They can be frozen for future use, cut into bite-size squares and served as cocktail snacks, or turned into a melty, hot meal by frying them in butter. (Dip cheese sandwiches into a mixture of egg and milk and fry as for French toast, and you have a feast.)

We aren't talking about plastic cheese slices on white sandwich bread. Use the best whole-grain bread and a good cheese, such as Vermont sharp cheddar. Butter the bread, if you like, then spread liberally with a grainy or Dijon-style mustard.

Additional items, such as sliced tomatoes, lettuce, meat, or mayonnaise, should be added later, just before serving. If you stick to the basic recipe of bread, butter, mustard, and cheese, these sandwiches will keep a day or two without refrigeration or fear of spoilage.

Make your own cracker snacks. Place ready-made pie crust on a cookie sheet, score it very lightly into wedges, and sprinkle it with seasoned salt, sesame seeds, or poppy seeds. Bake at 400°F until brown.

Veggie Cheese Melt Sandwiches

12 ounces mushrooms, cleaned and sliced
$^1/_2$ stick butter, melted
2 cups thinly sliced vegetables (sweet peppers, zucchini, yellow squash, cabbage, or some bean sprouts)

1 large onion, sliced into rings
soy sauce
16 ounces grated sharp cheddar cheese
10 slices bread, lightly buttered

Set out half the bread and sprinkle evenly with half the grated cheese. Sauté mushrooms in butter in a large skillet, adding and stir-frying other vegetables over medium heat until everything is crisp-tender. Season with several splashes of soy sauce. Top bread with well-drained hot vegetables, remaining cheese, and another slice of bread. Cover with a clean dishtowel for a few minutes so the heat of the vegetables melts the cheese, then cut sandwiches in half and serve. Makes 5 sandwiches.

Passing Lane Sandwich Puffs

When you're out of bread, make elegant sandwiches by rustling up a batch of cream puffs.

1 stick butter
1 cup water
1 cup flour
4 eggs

sandwiches and snacks

Bring butter and water to a boil and remove from heat. Dump in flour all at once and mix. Continue mixing over very low flame, stirring constantly, and add eggs one at a time, to make a thick dough. Drop by tablespoons onto a greased baking sheet and bake at 400°F for 10 minutes, then 350°F for about 25 minutes more. Dough should lose its shiny look and appear dry. Let cool in the oven with the door ajar. Fill with sandwich filling such as chicken, tuna, or ham salad. Makes 8 to 10 puffs.

Variations: Add a teaspoon of Dijon mustard and ½ cup grated cheese to the dough. Instead of forming individual puffs, dough can be spread in a circle or dropped by tablespoons to form a ring. Cut the entire piece in half horizontally, fill with sandwich makings, then slice into wedges.

To make cocktail snacks, make smaller puffs by the teaspoon and stuff with your favorite filling.

Battered Sandwiches

This works best with sandwich fillings that hold together well with the bread, such as ham or chicken salad or a filling bound with grated cheese (which melts as it cooks, cementing the ingredients).

4 sandwiches (chicken salad, cheese spread, tuna, etc.)
1 cup pancake mix
1 egg
1 cup milk
oil

Cut sandwiches in half. Whisk together pancake mix, egg, and milk and dip each sandwich in the batter, coating thoroughly so none of the filling is exposed. (It could spit and spatter during cooking.) Heat 1 or 2 inches of oil in a roomy skillet and fry sandwiches until they are crispy and brown. Drain on paper towel. Careful when taking the first bite! The filling is sealed in, bursting with heat and steam. Makes 4 sandwiches.

sandwiches and snacks

Pit-Stop Pasties

2 tubes (8 each) refrigerated crescent rolls
4 ounces grated cheese
12 ounces deli ham salad

Separate rolls into triangles. Mix ham salad with cheese and divide among half of the triangles. Top carefully with other half of triangles. Seal each pasty by moistening edges with water and pressing securely. Cut a small slit in tops so steam can escape. Bake on a greased cookie sheet in a 350°F oven for 10 to 15 minutes or until golden. Makes 8 pasties.

"Crab" Salad Pockets

8 ounces imitation crabmeat
1 tablespoon lemon juice
1 rib celery, diced
2 to 3 scallions, sliced
1 8-ounce can crushed pineapple, well drained
$1/4$ cup slivered almonds
mayonnaise
$1/2$ teaspoon curry powder (or to taste)
avocado
4 pitas

Buy imitation crabmeat that is fully cooked and ready to eat, and shred or chop it in a small bowl. Splash with lemon juice. Add celery, scallions, pineapple, curry powder, and almonds, and enough mayonnaise to bind mixture. Divide into pita bread halves and garnish each with a slice of ripe avocado. Makes 4 pockets.

When you're out of celery, add crunch to sandwich fillings by using diced canned water chestnuts, well drained and diced.

sandwiches and snacks

Onion Pie

3 jumbo sweet onions, thinly
   sliced
$\frac{1}{2}$ stick butter
1 9-inch unbaked pie shell
16 ounces cottage cheese

2 eggs
$\frac{1}{2}$ teaspoon salt
dash pepper
dash nutmeg

Sauté onions in butter until limp. Prick pie shell with a fork and bake 5 minutes at 425°F. Put half the well-drained onions in pie shell. Whisk together eggs, cottage cheese, and seasonings, pour over onions, then top with remaining onions. Bake at 350°F until crust is browned and cheese mixture is set. Let stand 5 minutes before cutting. Serve in wedges as a snack or appetizer. Serves 8 as an appetizer or 4 as a main course.

Scurry Curry Chicken Sandwiches

2 5-ounce cans chunk chicken
$\frac{1}{2}$ cup raisins
$\frac{1}{2}$ cup chopped peanuts
1 to 2 teaspoons (to taste) curry powder
1 large rib celery, diced
mayonnaise
16 slices bread
butter

Shred chicken in a bowl and mix in remaining ingredients with enough mayonnaise to bind. Spread on buttered bread to make 8 sandwiches.

sandwiches and snacks

Chicken McSpeedSnack

Start with fully-cooked chicken nuggets from a supermarket or fast-food restaurant. To reheat in the oven, spread them in a single layer on a lightly greased baking sheet and bake 5 minutes at 425°F. Serve with hot (from the microwave) and cold dipping sauces, such as the following:

◆ Whisk together ½ cup plain yogurt, ½ cup mayonnaise, and 1 teaspoon each dried dill weed and pickle relish.

◆ Heat a jar of pineapple ice cream topping with 1 tablespoon Dijon mustard.

◆ Heat a 10-ounce jar of orange marmalade with 2 to 3 tablespoons soy sauce.

◆ Whisk together ½ cup applesauce with ½ cup blueberry preserves and 1 tablespoon lemon juice. Microwave on High 20 seconds at a time, stirring until warm and well blended. Or use baby food strained plums with plum jelly and a dollop of Dijon-style mustard.

◆ Mix equal parts of sour cream and salsa.

◆ Stir together ½ cup honey with 2 tablespoons Dijon mustard. Serve hot or cold.

◆ Stir 1 teaspoon curry powder (more to taste) into 1 cup nonfat lemon yogurt.

South Pacific Sandwiches

2 cups diced cooked chicken
mayonnaise
pinch curry powder
½ teaspoon ground ginger
4 hoagie buns
⅓ cup flaked coconut

sandwiches and snacks

Mix chicken with curry powder and ginger and add enough mayonnaise to moisten. Scoop out a generous, full-length trench in each bun (put aside excess bread for another use or to feed the birds). Pile filling into buns and sprinkle generously with coconut, pressing it into the filling. Bake on a greased cookie sheet at 400°F until heated through and crusty, about 7 to 10 minutes. Makes 4 hoagies.

Sandwiches Crab Louis

6 to 8 hot-dog buns
butter
$\frac{1}{2}$ cup chili sauce or salsa
1 cup mayonnaise
2 hard-boiled eggs, diced
3 cups cooked crab or lobster meat

Slice buns and open just enough to butter the insides, then toast in a 425°F oven just until brown. Mix together chili sauce and mayo, then fold in eggs and seafood and pile into toasted buns. Makes 6 to 8 sandwiches.

Tuna Bean Sandwiches

1 15- or 16-ounce can white beans
2 tablespoons olive oil
2 tablespoons lemon juice
1 small sweet onion, minced
1 can or pouch solid-pack tuna (about 3 ounces)
2 tablespoons fresh minced parsley
bread or rolls for 4 to 6 sandwiches

Drain beans and mash them slightly while adding olive oil and lemon juice. Add onion, parsley (don't substitute dried), and tuna, breaking it up as you mix. Spread on bread. Makes 4 to 6 sandwiches.

sandwiches and snacks

Just for fun, make miniature hot dogs, using finger rolls and cocktail wieners or sausages, and provide ketchup, mustard, and relish for trimming.

"Crab"wiches

4 English muffins, split and toasted
$1/2$ green pepper, finely diced
2 to 3 ribs celery, diced
4 to 5 scallions, finely sliced
1 tablespoon butter
16 ounces imitation crabmeat, chopped
2 tablespoons mayonnaise
1 tablespoon lemon juice
1 1-ounce packet Hollandaise sauce mix

Sauté vegetables in butter in a nonstick skillet. Then add crabmeat and sauté just to heat thoroughly. Stir in mayonnaise and place some of the mixture on each English muffin half. Prepare Hollandaise sauce according to package directions and pour over crabwiches. Makes 4 sandwiches.

Muffulettas

This is a New Orleans street sandwich, as popular a walking meal as it is a sit-down sandwich in sidewalk cafés. For the RV cook it provides a feast of a sandwich that is made ahead and improves with chilling, so it's ideal to keep in the refrigerator and bring out for a rushed roadside lunch.

1 16-ounce jar mixed marinated vegetables
2 cloves garlic, peeled
6 stuffed olives, sliced
1 tablespoon olive oil
1 unsliced loaf French bread
4 ounces sliced salami
4 ounces sliced provolone cheese

A day or two ahead, add garlic cloves to jar of vegetables and put jar in refrigerator. To complete, drain vegetables well, discard garlic, and chop vegetables coarsely. Drain again. Cut loaf in half and dig out some of the bread. (Save for another purpose such as making breadcrumbs or bread pudding.) Brush cut side of bread very lightly with olive oil and sprinkle bottom half with half the vegetables plus some of the sliced olives. Top with overlapping slices of salami and provolone, the remaining vegetables and olives, then the other half of the loaf. Slice into 4 to 6 sandwiches and wrap each tightly in plastic wrap. Chill several hours or overnight.

Sausage-Stuffed Baguettes

These can be assembled at home, in advance of a weekend trip, then baked hot and crusty during a quick roadside stop. Don't forget to pick up the bread at the deli when you get the other ingredients. And choose the best, leanest sausage in the store.

1 pound pork sausage
4 ounces smoked ham, diced
1 cup ricotta cheese
1 10-ounce package chopped spinach, thawed and drained
1 egg, lightly beaten
1/4 cup thinly sliced green onion
2 22-inch baguettes or 6 8-inch French rolls
olive oil

Fry and drain sausage. Squeeze any excess moisture from spinach. Place spinach in a mixing bowl and mix in remaining ingredients except bread. Refrigerate while slicing bread or rolls in half lengthwise. Scoop out some of the filling (save it for breadcrumbs) and brush very lightly with olive oil. Fill with sausage mixture. Put halves back together and wrap in foil. Chill at once. To serve, peel back some of foil to expose the bread so it will get crisp and bake at 375°F about 30 to 40 minutes. The filling must be thoroughly heated so the egg cooks and the cheese "sets." Makes 6 sandwiches.

Microwave Reubens

Assemble and wrap these at home a day or two ahead of time. A few minutes in your microwave will heat them up fresh, piquant, and delicious. The quantities below are only suggestions; you may use more or less, depending on whether you like thick or thin sandwiches.

8 slices beefsteak rye bread
butter
$1/2$ pound lean corned beef, thinly sliced
8 ounces sauerkraut, well drained
Thousand Island dressing
sliced Swiss cheese

Toast bread and butter it so it doesn't get soggy. Layer one slice with corned beef, sauerkraut, dressing, Swiss cheese, and finish with another slice of corned beef. Top with a second slice of bread, butter side in. Wrap individually in microwave-safe wrap and refrigerate. To serve, microwave each sandwich on High for about 45 seconds, until cheese is melted and sandwich is heated through. Makes 4 sandwiches.

Variation: Place sandwiches on a lightly greased cookie sheet, spray tops with olive oil, and top with a second cookie sheet weighted with a clean, heavy pot or skillet. Bake at 400°F until crusty.

Creamy Clam Spread

1 6-ounce can minced clams, drained
1 can condensed cream of chicken soup
8 ounces cream cheese, at room temperature
$1/4$ cup ketchup
1 small sweet onion, diced

Mash everything together with a fork or with an electric mixer until well mixed. Spread on crackers for snacks or make sandwiches by spreading generously on buttered bread. Top with a lettuce leaf. Makes $2^{1}/2$ cups.

sandwiches and snacks

Nosebags

Many types of trail mixes are available, or you can invent your own. To achieve a balanced trail "meal," maximize low-sugar and sugar-free cereals (round oat cereal, bite-size shredded wheat, Chex), minimize fat (nuts, seeds, chocolate bits), and don't overdo the sugar (Gummi Bears, marshmallows, jellybeans).

Here is a very sweet version. Take it as a walking dessert on a long hike after a big meal.

1/2 cup toasted pecan or walnut halves
1/2 cup toasted sunflower seeds
1/2 cup canned or packaged grated coconut

1/2 cup banana chips
2 cups mixed dried fruit (pitted prunes, dried cranberries, dried apricots, raisins), large pieces cut up

Combine all ingredients. Measure 1-cup portions into zip-top snack bags and hit the trail. Makes 4 nosebags.

Texican Two-Step

Step 1 is to create this tangy dip. Step 2 is to dive in with crisp tortilla chips and eat it by the scoop!

16 ounces bulk sausage
1 10-ounce package frozen chopped spinach, thawed and drained
1 10- to 14-ounce can diced tomatoes with chilis

8 ounces cream cheese, cut up
1 tablespoon water
4 ounces grated cheddar cheese
3 to 4 scallions, sliced
hot sauce to taste

sandwiches and snacks

In large saucepan, break up and fry sausage until it's no longer pink. Squeeze any excess moisture from spinach. Stir in spinach and tomatoes and heat through. Lower heat and gradually stir in cream cheese and water until a creamy sauce forms. Turn off heat and stir in cheese and scallions until cheese melts. Season to taste. Serve at once. Makes $3\frac{1}{2}$ cups.

Customize this dip by using low- or nonfat cheese, hot or mild sausage, or even vegetarian sausage.

It should be served hot, so if you've made it ahead and refrigerated it, nuke it for a few minutes on Medium before serving.

Poor Folks' Pâté

This is a healthful alternative to junk-food snacking. It's a breeze to make at home in your food processor, so make enough for a week. Then press it into containers, cover, and keep cold. Serve with healthful rye crackers.

1 medium onion, chopped
1 tablespoon virgin olive oil
1 15- or 16-ounce can green beans, drained
2 hard-boiled eggs, quartered
$\frac{1}{4}$ cup toasted sunflower seeds
2 tablespoons sherry
$\frac{1}{8}$ teaspoon nutmeg
freshly ground pepper
1 to 2 tablespoons mayonnaise

Sauté onion in oil until tender, then process with beans, eggs, and sunflower seeds. Mix in sherry, nutmeg, and pepper and add just enough mayo to bind. The mixture should be stiff. Makes about $1\frac{1}{2}$ cups.

To use up leftover sandwiches, arrange them loosely in a buttered baking dish and mix up enough eggs and milk (1 egg for each 1 cup milk) to cover completely. Refrigerate several hours or overnight, then bake at 350°F until set like custard and serve as a casserole.

sandwiches and snacks

Bacon Wraps

1 pound bacon

Fillings
water chestnuts
watermelon-rind pickles
artichoke hearts, cut in half
whole oysters
chicken livers, cut in half
fresh pineapple, cut into chunks
fresh apple, cut into wedges
broccoli or cauliflower florets, parboiled
giant stuffed olives

Cut bacon slices in half and wrap each around the filling(s) of your choice. Fasten with a toothpick and bake at 375°F for about 15 minutes or until bacon is done. Drain on paper towels, then transfer to a serving plate. Makes about 30 wraps.

Popcorn Olé

Start with unsalted, low- or nonfat popcorn and add your own South-western spin. This zesty snack is delicious with hot cider, cold lemonade, or icy margaritas.

$1/2$ stick butter, melted
$1 1/2$ teaspoons chili powder
$1/2$ teaspoon salt
1 tablespoon lime juice
1 teaspoon fresh lime zest
$1/4$ teaspoon cayenne pepper
1 3-ounce bag microwave popcorn, popped
up to 2 cups roasted, salted peanuts, mixed nuts, or pepitas (optional)

Stir seasonings into butter. Put hot popcorn (and nuts) in a large bowl, drizzle with butter mixture, and toss well to coat. Makes 6 cups.

sandwiches and snacks

Shortcut Soft Pretzels

If you have frozen bread dough on hand, bring it out on a rainy day and let the children work the dough and tie the knots. If you have coarse salt on hand, so much the better. Butter-flavored popcorn salt is also a good choice, or just use regular salt.

1 loaf frozen bread dough, defrosted
1 egg
1 tablespoon water

Divide loaf into 16 pieces. Roll each piece between your hands to form a long rope, then tie into knotlike shapes. (If this is a family project, you might even turn it into a knot-tying contest.) Place on greased baking sheets and let rise until double. Beat egg and water together and brush on pretzels. Sprinkle with salt and bake at 375°F for 10 to 15 minutes or until evenly browned. Makes 16 pretzels.

"Real" pretzels are boiled before baking, so these will have a lighter and more breadlike texture, but slather them with yellow mustard and nobody will care.

Fast Lane

◆ Melt 3 tablespoons butter, add 1 tablespoon minced garlic, and 1½ teaspoons Tabasco. Cook 1 minute. Toss with 3 cups pecan halves and spread on a baking sheet. Bake for 1 hour at 250°F, stirring occasionally. Cool and serve as a hot and spicy cocktail snack.

◆ Make a fiery, low-fat dip by combining 1 cup yogurt, 2 cups cottage cheese, ½ cup chopped red onion, 2½ teaspoons cumin, and ½ teaspoon Tabasco in a blender. Blend until smooth, add another ¼ teaspoon Tabasco if you want more kick, chill, and serve with raw vegetables.

◆ Rediscover apple butter as a satiny sandwich spread. It glides on more evenly than most jellies and combines deliciously with peanut butter, sliced bananas, crumbled bacon, or spreadable cream cheese.

sandwiches and snacks

◆ Add zest to a sliced turkey sandwich by spreading it with mayo, then cranberry-orange relish.

◆ Add milk to biscuit mix to make a thick batter. Dip slices of banana, apple, or other firm, fresh fruit, and deep-fry until crusty brown. Serve as a snack with syrup or powdered sugar.

◆ Shave calories by using nonfat sour cream in dips.

◆ To make a quick, low-fat dip for raw vegetables, stir 1 teaspoon curry powder (more to taste) into a carton of lemon yogurt.

◆ Make nachos with frozen french fries, browned hot and crisp in the oven, instead of tortilla chips.

◆ To turn toasted cheese sandwiches into a knife and fork meal, heat a can of broccoli cheese soup with $1/4$ cup milk in the microwave on High for 3 to 5 minutes. Stir and spoon over hot and crusty sandwiches.

◆ Use diced fennel root as part of the celery measurement in chicken salad sandwich filling.

sandwiches and snacks

Eight

Menu Makers: Meat and Poultry

For more recipes utilizing meat, see the chapters on One-Dish Meals, Soups, Light My Fire!, and Anytime Foods.

Peanut Sauce Lamb Satay

This recipe comes from the American Lamb Council. If you're tired of the same old grilled meats, try this exciting blend of flavors. Do the first steps at home and keep the meat, marinating in a plastic bag, in your RV refrigerator to use the first day out. Based on an Indonesian recipe that calls for hot pepper, this one is milder. If you like, add your favorite hot pepper to the peanut sauce.

about 20 ounces boneless
    lamb leg, well trimmed
$1/2$ cup lime juice

Sauce
5 tablespoons creamy peanut
    butter
drained pineapple juice

Garnish
1 20-ounce can pineapple
    chunks (juice reserved)

Cut lamb into bite-size chunks and put it and lime juice in plastic bag. Refrigerate several hours or overnight. To proceed, drain meat, pat dry, and thread on skewers. (If you're using bamboo skewers, soak them in water for an hour first.) Broil over well-started coals 6 to 7 minutes, turning once.

To make sauce, put peanut butter in a small saucepan over low heat. Gradually stir in pineapple juice. Cook and stir until hot and smooth.

To serve, garnish meat with pineapple chunks and give each person a small cup of peanut sauce for dipping. Serves 4.

Complete the meal with fruited rice, a tangy salad, soft breadsticks, and plain butter cookies with jasmine tea.

Individual Beef Wellingtons

4 4- to 8-ounce filets mignons, partially frozen
1 package puff pastry, thawed
1 8-ounce can liver paté
1 egg, beaten

Sprinkle filets with salt and pepper and sear in a very hot skillet just until brown on the outside but still raw inside. "Frost" each on top with liver paté. Roll out puff pastry and cut 4 pieces large enough to wrap filets. (Scraps can be baked separately to eat later with jam.) Wrap filets completely and seal edges with a fingertip dipped in water. Place on a sprayed baking sheet seam side down and brush with egg. Bake 20 to 30 minutes at 425°F until pastry is golden. Serves 4.

Serve at once with mesclun salad, steamed broccoli, buttered carrots, and stemmed sweet cherries with a chocolate dip for dessert.

Quick Curried Pork

The secret to developing the flavor of curry powder is to sauté it in oil before liquids are added. The secret to the quick cooking of this stir-fry is to slice the pork thinly, slanting across the grain. This is easier if the meat is partially frozen first. I sometimes do this step at home the day before and carry the sliced pork (sealed in a plastic bag) in the coldest spot in the refrigerator.

meat and poultry

1 pound lean boneless pork,
  partially frozen
2 tablespoons oil
1 rib celery, diced
$^1/_2$ red pepper, diced
$^1/_2$ green pepper, diced
2 to 3 scallions, diced

2 tablespoons curry powder
  (or to taste)
2 tablespoons cornstarch
1 $^1/_2$ cups water
1 chicken bouillon cube
1 10-ounce package frozen
  peas, thawed

Slice pork in thin rings. In a roomy skillet brown pork in oil. Continue stir-frying while adding vegetables, then curry powder. Make a paste of the cornstarch and a bit of the water. When pork is no longer pink and vegetables are crisp-tender, add cornstarch mixture and the rest of the water. Stir in chicken bouillon cube and cook, stirring frequently, over medium heat until the sauce is thick and clear. Stir in the peas and heat through. Serves 4.

Complete the meal with white rice, a jellied apple salad, cinnamon apple tea, and coconut custard pie.

Pork Chop Bake

6 lean pork chops
6 tart baking apples, such as Granny Smith
$^1/_3$ to $^1/_2$ cup raisins
$^1/_3$ to $^1/_2$ cup chopped walnuts
maple syrup
2 pounds sauerkraut

Brown pork chops well on both sides in a nonstick skillet. Rinse and drain sauerkraut and spread in a large, shallow baking pan or oven-to-table baking dish. Core apples, pare a strip of peel from around the top, and fill apples with mixed raisins and nuts. Arrange pork chops and apples atop sauerkraut, drizzle apples with syrup, and bake at 350°F for about 45 minutes or until apples are done. Serves 6.

Complete the meal with buttered mashed potatoes, rye rolls, and fresh nectarines for dessert.

meat and poultry

Pork Chop Skillet

4 lean boneless pork chops
4 canned pineapple rings
   (reserve juice)
4 slices green pepper

4 dried apricot halves
4 pitted dried prunes
sherry or marsala wine

In a roomy skillet brown pork chops on both sides. Reduce heat. Top each chop with a pineapple ring and then a green pepper slice. In the center of each chop place a prune stuffed with an apricot. Add juice from the canned pineapple, cover, and braise over low heat about 20 minutes or until chops are tender and done through. Remove chops from pan and arrange on plates. Boil away excess cooking liquid, deglaze pan with sherry or marsala wine, and drizzle over chops. Serves 4.

Serve with stovetop-style cornbread dressing, steamed broccoli, and Temple oranges for dessert.

Variation: Try ½-inch-thick rings cut from seeded acorn squash instead of the pineapple and green pepper and use water instead of pineapple juice.

Fruited Chicken

8 skinless chicken thighs
2 tablespoons olive oil
1 can condensed cream of
   chicken soup
¾ cup orange juice
1 large onion, diced
2 cloves garlic, minced

2 tablespoons slivered
   almonds
2 tablespoons raisins
¼ teaspoon apple pie spice
¼ teaspoon turmeric
fresh orange sections
hot rice

In a large skillet brown chicken in oil and pour off excess fat. Whisk together soup and orange juice and pour over chicken. Sprinkle with onion, garlic, almonds, raisins, and seasonings. Cover and simmer over low-medium flame for 45 minutes or until chicken is tender. Place chicken on serving plates atop a bed of hot rice. Stir sauce and pour over chicken. Garnish with orange sections. Serves 4 to 6.

This goes well with tiny green peas, carrot-cabbage slaw, a fruity quick bread such as cranberry loaf, and a light, lemony dessert.

meat and poultry

Chicken Rice Pot Pie

The next time you have leftover rice and chicken at home, bag and freeze them to make this on your next RV trip. If you like, the entire pie can be put together at home the night before. Just keep it well refrigerated until you bake it.

pastry for 2-crust, 9-inch pie
1 medium onion, diced
2 cloves garlic, minced
2 ribs celery, diced
2 tablespoons butter
1 can condensed cream of
　chicken soup

$1/3$ cup milk
$1^1/2$ cups diced, cooked
　chicken (or 2 6-ounce cans
　chunk chicken)
1 tablespoon lemon juice
$1^1/2$ cups cooked rice
4 hard-boiled eggs, sliced

Line a pie pan with one crust. Sauté onion, garlic, and celery in butter until softened, then mix in soup, milk, chicken, and lemon juice. Alternate layers of rice, sliced eggs, and the chicken mixture in the pan, then add the top crust, seal, trim edges, and flute. Bake at 375°F until brown. (Cooking time will vary: If made ahead and chilled in the refrigerator, the pie will take as long as 1 hour. If freshly made with hot filling, it will brown in as little as 35 to 45 minutes.) For easier serving, let stand 5 to 10 minutes before cutting. Serves 6 to 8.

Complete the meal with a big platter of raw vegetables, whole-cranberry sauce, and a "walking" dessert such as Nestlé caramel crunch bars or crisp apples to enjoy on a sunset birdwatching hike.

Microwave Turkey Divan

Don't buy cheap, chopped-and-formed deli turkey for this dish. Buy real roasted turkey breast and have it sliced to order so it's not too thin, not too thick.

1 10-ounce package frozen
　broccoli florets, thawed
8 slices roasted turkey breast
1 can condensed cream of
　chicken soup

pinch nutmeg
4 tablespoons dry white wine
6 ounces grated cheddar or
　Monterey Jack cheese

meat and poultry

Overlap 2 slices of turkey and place 1 or 2 florets on them. Roll up and place, seam side down, in a microware dish that has a cover. Repeat with remaining turkey and broccoli. Combine soup, wine, nutmeg, and cheese in a 1-quart microwave cooking container and cook on High for 2 minutes. Pour over turkey rolls, cover dish, and cook on High 8 to 10 minutes, rotating once, until heated and bubbly. Let stand a few minutes before serving. Serves 4.

Complete the meal with microwave-baked potatoes, a green salad, monkey bread, and a dessert of instant vanilla pudding drowning in frozen strawberries thawed to slushiness.

Pollo Pot Pie

Put a cornbread sombrero on this favorite, and you have a winning combination!

2 10-ounce cans chunk chicken	about $1/3$ cup water (or use juice from corn)
3 carrots, cut up	1 8-ounce can corn, drained
1 rib celery, cut up	1 cup frozen peas, thawed
1 large potato, scrubbed and diced	1 4-ounce can diced green chilis, drained
$1/2$ teaspoon freshly ground pepper	1 box Jiffy cornbread mix
1 tablespoon cornstarch or instant-blend flour	

Empty chicken (with juice) into a saucepan and break up. Add carrots, celery, and potato. Cover and simmer over low heat until vegetables are tender. Stir in pepper. Mix cornstarch or flour with enough water to make a paste. Stir into chicken mixture and cook over medium heat until it thickens. Add more water if needed to make a gravy-like sauce. Stir in corn, peas, and chilis. Divide mixture among 6 individual casserole dishes. Don't overfill. Prepare cornbread batter according to package directions and pour some onto each casserole dish. Bake at 400°F about 10 minutes, until cornbread is set and crust is light brown. Serves 6.

If you want to make this in one large casserole dish, cooking time will be about 12 to 15 minutes.

meat and poultry

Cut leftover meatloaf or salmon loaf into serving-size chunks and wrap each in thawed puff pastry dough, rolled as thin as possible. Bake at 425°F until brown and serve with a simple sauce made by stirring fresh or dried dill into a mixture of half mayo and half yogurt.

Janet's Chicken and Dumplings

This is a comfort food classic I serve at least once a week when we're on the go. By cooking vegetables with the chicken, I make a complete meal in one pot, and the vegetables make for a richer gravy. Throw in a handful of thawed peas and some chopped parsley just before serving and the dish will be even more colorful.

4 servings chicken (such as skinless thighs, bone-in breasts, or canned)
4 carrots, cut into chunks
1 medium onion, cut up
2 cloves garlic
3 ribs celery, sliced
1 cup frozen peas, thawed (optional)

handful chopped fresh parsley (optional)

Dumplings
1 1/2 cups biscuit mix
water or milk

If you're using canned chicken, bone it and place in a roomy pot with the garlic. If chicken is fresh, brown it and garlic in a little olive oil. Then add a few inches of water and the carrots, onion, and celery. Cover and simmer while stirring up the dumplings.

Add liquid to biscuit mix to make a stiff dough and drop by heaping tablespoons (you should end up with 8 dumplings) atop the boiling liquid. Keep the liquid boiling 10 minutes, uncovered (make sure pot doesn't boil dry), then cover pot, lower flame, and cook 10 minutes more without peeking. If using, stir in peas and top with parsley, then serve at once. (Dumplings get soggy if they are kept waiting.) Serves 4.

meat and poultry

Stovetop Meatloaf and Baked Potatoes

When you want a quick meatloaf without having to heat the oven, try this crusty, fragrant skillet loaf and browned potatoes. This can also be made in a Dutch oven in the campfire or on a grill over well-started coals.

1 pound lean ground beef	1 egg
2 tablespoons dried onion flakes	2 large baking potatoes, halved
1 teaspoon salt	1 can condensed cream of mushroom soup (optional)
dash pepper	
1/3 cup rolled oats	

Smoosh meatloaf makings together in a plastic freezer bag (regular bags are thin and may tear) until well mixed (you won't have to wash a bowl). Turn out into a cold, lightly greased, heavy skillet (preferably cast aluminum) that has a heavy, tight-fitting lid. Discard the bag. Shape meatloaf into a mound in the center of the skillet, leaving room around the edges for potatoes. Place potatoes cut side down in the skillet. Cover and bake (don't peek more than once or twice; stovetop baking relies on an even envelope of heat) over a medium-low flame 45 to 60 minutes. Serves 4.

If you want gravy, stir the mushroom soup into the pan drippings with a little water or red wine until heated through.

For a complete meal, add crusty rolls and a leafy salad glistening with cheesy vinaigrette dressing.

Springtime Ham Rolls

Because you buy the ham in the deli, it's fully cooked and sliced to order. I can have this on the table 20 minutes after we've hooked up at the campground.

8 or 10 fresh asparagus spears	2 tablespoons seasoned bread-crumbs
6 slices deli-baked ham	
2 tablespoons oil	2 tablespoons grated cheddar
1 tablespoon minced garlic	

Wash and trim asparagus and sauté in hot oil with garlic until asparagus is just crisp-tender. While it's cooking, lay ham in overlapping slices to form 2 rectangles. Arrange asparagus in bundles on ham. Fry breadcrumbs in remaining oil and bits of garlic and sprinkle over asparagus. Top each with a tuft of cheese. Roll up and place, seam side down, on a microware dish or baking pan. Microwave on High, turning every 30 seconds, until heated through or bake 10 minutes at 350°F. Serves 2; can be easily multiplied to feed any number of happy campers.

Complete the menu with deli coleslaw, slabs of hot cornbread with honey butter, and mugs of hot cranberry tea.

Variation: Serve rolls in buttered and toasted hero sandwich buns.

Boneless Roast Bonanza Sauce

If you have to serve a crowd out of your small oven, get a boneless roast. Roast according to cookbook directions for lamb, pork, or whatever, and smother it with this sauce.

1 red pepper, diced	1 tablespoon cornstarch
1 green pepper, diced	1 tablespoon vinegar
1 medium onion, diced	2 teaspoons sugar
1 8-ounce can mandarin oranges	splash Worcestershire sauce
1 8-ounce can crushed pineapple	2 tablespoons sherry

Drain pineapple and oranges into a saucepan or microwave container and add vinegar, Worcestershire sauce, and sherry. Gradually mix in the cornstarch, add remaining ingredients, and cook, stirring frequently, until thick and clear. Pour over roast for last 45 minutes of baking time. Makes about $1\frac{1}{2}$ cups.

Try using graham cracker crumbs instead of breadcrumbs in ham loaf.

Ginger Chicken

You'll need hot rice for the finished presentation, so plan ahead to prepare regular or instant white or brown rice.

4 slices bacon, diced
1 teaspoon curry powder
   (or to taste)
1 large onion, diced
2 teaspoons minced garlic
1 cup water
1 chicken bouillon cube

4 boneless chicken breast
   halves
2 teaspoons ginger
4 firm bananas, cut into
   chunks
2 hard-boiled eggs, chopped
$1/3$ cup raisins

Fry bacon in a large skillet until crisp, then pour off all but about 1 tablespoon of the fat. Add curry powder, onion, and garlic and sauté until limp, then add water and bouillon cube. Stir to dissolve. Lay chicken flat, sprinkle with ginger, and form into bundles. Place chicken bundles atop the hot sauce in the skillet, then ladle more sauce over them. Cover and simmer over low flame 10 minutes, then baste again and add bananas, eggs, and raisins. Cover and cook 10 minutes more or until chicken is done. Arrange a bed of rice on each plate, top with chicken, and ladle on some sauce. Serves 4.

Steak Port Antonio

This recipe was developed by the people who make Tabasco sauce. Let's name names: There is no substitute for the original Tabasco sauce. I make this sauce in a small, nonstick skillet.

4 servings of your favorite cut of steak

Sauce
$1/4$ cup rum
1 tablespoon chopped shallots
1 stick butter
2 teaspoons lime juice
$1/2$ teaspoon Tabasco sauce
1 tablespoon chopped parsley

meat and poultry

To make sauce, combine rum and shallots, bring to a boil, and simmer 2 minutes. Stir in remaining ingredients and return to a boil. Turn off heat and cover to keep warm. Broil or grill steaks, place on serving plates, and spoon on sauce. Serves 4.

Complete the menu with campfire-baked sweet potatoes, boil-in-the-bag vegetables, buttercrunch lettuce salad, and Atkins Endulge candy bars for dessert while you take a stroll.

Newer Skewers

Kebobs are the quickest and most versatile way to barbecue. Here are some ideas to string you along.

◆ Alternate chunks of light and dark sausages.

◆ Weave strips of boneless chicken breast with small pieces of highly spiced sausage. The bland chicken tames the sausage and the fatty sausage bastes the dry chicken.

◆ Make surf-and-turfbobs by threading parboiled chunks of boneless, skinless chicken breast with whole shrimp or chunks of lobster. (Parboiled chicken cooks faster, so you don't overcook the delicate seafood.)

The Magic of Marinade

The outdoor grill is the RV cook's second stove, and many RV families cook every dinner outdoors. To become an expert barbecue chef is not easy. By using marinades you can assure more reliable flavor and tenderness.

An entire cookbook can be filled with recipes for marinades, but the truth is that they boil down to certain basics according to their country of origin. Here, from the National Pork Producers Council, is a summary of the flavors that go into each type of marinade. Because the flavors steal so subtly into the meat, and their intensity depends as much on the length of the marinating as on the strength of the spices, amounts can be fairly flexible—using, of course, your own good judgment about proportions. In each case the chief ingredient is listed first. Use enough to coat the meat well. Other ingredients are added in smaller amounts. Marinating is best done in a well-sealed plastic bag that can be turned and tumbled repeatedly for even distribution of flavors.

◆ Caribbean: lime juice, oregano, thyme, allspice

◆ Indian: yogurt, crushed ginger and garlic, ground coriander, cumin, turmeric, red pepper

◆ Mediterranean: wine or vinegar, olive oil, garlic, oregano, rosemary

◆ Asian: soy sauce, garlic, ginger, sesame oil

◆ Southwestern: cider vinegar, onion, ground chili, cumin, oregano

◆ Scandinavian: oil, lemon, dill or cardamom

Basic marinade safety rules:

◆ Meat should always be refrigerated while marinating.

◆ Once raw meat has been in a marinade, the marinade should never be used unless it's cooked thoroughly. Use it to baste the meat as it cooks, or cook and serve as a sauce with the meat. If you bring raw meat to the grill on a platter, wash the platter thoroughly before using it to serve the cooked meat.

◆ Don't marinate meat in a metal container. The metal could react with the marinade ingredients and impart an "off" color or flavor.

◆ Marinades with high-sugar ingredients such as honey or ketchup tend to carbonize sooner when cooked so meats and poultry that require long, thorough cooking are best basted with sweet sauces toward the end of their cooking time.

Minimum–Maximum Meat Marinating Times

strips, thin chops	30 minutes–2 hours
cubes for kebobs	1–24 hours
thick chops	2–24 hours
bone-in roasts, 4–12 pounds	12–14 hours
dry-rub ribs	12–24 hours
boneless roasts, 1–5 pounds	12–24 hours
boneless roasts, 5+ pounds	24–72 hours

Pork Chops Adobo

This is a simple recipe because it has only a few ingredients, but its flavors are rich and complex. The secret is the marinade, which can be easily started at home. Unlike most other recipes for marinated meats, this one calls for skillet cooking, so it's an ideal indoor barbecue. Flavor intensity increases with time, so marinate at least 4 hours.

4 lean, boneless pork loin chops
1 teaspoon oil

Marinade
1 12-ounce can or jar diced jalapeño peppers, undrained
4 teaspoons oregano
2 cloves garlic, crushed
2 teaspoons cumin
4 tablespoons cider vinegar

Combine marinade ingredients in a plastic bag and then add chops. Marinate 4 to 24 hours in the refrigerator. Discard marinade or boil 5 minutes and serve (very sparingly) as a sauce. Heat the oil in a nonstick skillet and fry chops 5 minutes on each side. Then cover and cook until the meat is done through. Serves 4.

Serve with cold broccoli vinaigrette, Mexicorn from a can, hot corn sticks, and a fresh fruit salad splashed with apple brandy for dessert.

meat and poultry

Panfastic Beef Stroganoff

The secret to the quick cooking of this tender stovetop Stroganoff is to slice the beef thinly, slanting across the grain. This is easier if the meat is partially frozen first. I sometimes do this step at home the day before and carry the sliced beef (sealed in a plastic bag) in the coldest spot in the refrigerator.

1 1/2 pounds lean top round
   or London broil
1 teaspoon oil
1 tablespoon instant-blend flour
1 teaspoon salt
dash pepper
1 8-ounce can mushrooms,
   drained (reserve juice)

1/2 cup liquid (water plus juice
   from the mushrooms)
1 medium onion, diced
1 tablespoon Dijon mustard
1/2 cup sour cream
minced parsley

Stir-fry steak slices in oil in a hot, nonstick skillet until browned. Stir flour into the liquid, then add mushrooms, salt, and pepper to the pan. Stir over medium flame until mixture thickens. Stir mustard into sour cream. Add to pan, cooking just until it's heated. Don't let it boil. Serve over instant mashed potatoes or rice and sprinkle with chopped parsley. Serves 6.

Complete the meal with boil-in-bag buttered peas and carrots and a slab of chilled tomato aspic. For dessert, pass out candy bar–size peppermint patties, grab the dog's leash, and go for a brisk walk.

Pantabulous Turkeyburgers

The ginger gives these burgers an exotic Asian tang. Pass the soy sauce at the table to bring out the taste even more.

1 pound lean ground turkey
1 small onion, minced
1 rib celery, minced
1 green pepper, minced
1 teaspoon salt (omit if you're
   serving soy sauce)

few bits candied ginger,
   minced
1/3 cup rolled oats
oil

Knead all ingredients together in a heavy-duty plastic bag. Rinse your hands in cold water and form meat into 4 patties. Fry in a little hot oil in a nonstick skillet until brown, then turn over, cover, and cook over medium flame until well browned on the other side and turkey is done through. Serves 4.

You can cover the patties to stay warm and set aside while you stir-fry a medley of your favorite cut-up vegetables in the same pan just until they're crisp-tender. Complete the meal with your favorite rice.

Skillet Spareribs

2 to 3 pounds lean baby spareribs, cut into pieces	salt, pepper
oil	*Marinade*
1 cup beef broth	1 cup white wine or grape juice
8 dried apricot halves	1 4- to 7-ounce jar baby food strained apricots
3 tablespoons cornstarch	
water	

Marinate ribs overnight in a mixture of wine and apricots in a heavy-duty plastic bag, turning from time to time. Drain ribs (reserve marinade), and brown on both sides in hot oil in a large skillet. Add reserved marinade, beef broth, and apricot halves. Cover and simmer until ribs are tender, about an hour. Mix cold water with the cornstarch to make a paste, then remove ribs and fruit from pan and pile them onto serving plates. Quickly stir the paste into the pan juices over a high flame until sauce is thickened and clear, adding more water or broth if necessary. Salt and pepper to taste. Spoon sauce over ribs and fruit. Serves 4.

Serve with steamed white rice (mix in 1 cup of thawed green peas for the last minute of cooking), a salad, and vanilla ice cream sauced with hot apple pie filling.

To spice up a boneless roast, stab randomly with an ice pick and force in peeled garlic cloves, raisins, and pistachios to various depths. They'll add flavor and, when the roast is sliced, will form an interesting mosaic pattern.

---

meat and poultry

To create a pattern in a meatloaf, add strips of cooked whole carrots and green beans when pressing the mixture into the pan. Or put half the meat in the pan, then add a line of hard-boiled eggs before topping with the rest of the meat mixture. Bake, let stand 10 minutes, turn out, and slice.

Schinken Schnitzel

This is a quick, easy way to make an old favorite. Start with fully cooked boiled ham, cut to order at the deli. Get the best quality, not chopped-and-formed lunch meat, and ask for thick slices.

8 thick slices (1 pound) boiled ham
2 eggs
2 tablespoons water
about 1 cup breadcrumbs
1 teaspoon thyme
1 tablespoon grated Parmesan cheese
oil

Cut each ham slice in half and pat dry with a paper towel. Beat together eggs and water and combine breadcrumbs, thyme, and cheese. Dip ham slices into egg mixture, then into the breadcrumb mixture. Fry in hot oil until brown and crispy. Serves 4 to 6.

Brown large batches of a mixture of ground meat, diced green and red peppers, onion, and garlic. Drain excess fat. Freeze mixture in 2-cup (1 pound) batches. It will be ready each time you make recipes that call for browned ground meat, onions, and peppers, such as One-Step Casserole on page 116 and Pizza Puff on page 120.

Nine

Seafood: Fishing for Compliments

Fishing and RV travel have been best buddies since the dawn of wheeled camping. In assembling these recipes I have kept in mind that some people fish to eat, some fish to release, and some buy their fish in markets in all its forms: cans, pouches, fresh, and frozen.

Even if you're an ardent and successful fisherman, I recommend keeping some canned or frozen seafood on hand for those times when you don't land as many fish as you'd planned. The best chowders and bouillabaisses are those made with a variety of flavors. By augmenting a small catch with canned or frozen shrimp, crab, oysters, mussels, or tuna, you can create a combination far more exotic and exciting than the plain fish meal you had planned to serve.

If you're grilling fish, there is no substitute for a grill basket. If you don't have one, you can also get a grip on a large, whole fish by making *foil girdles*. Tear off 2 sheets of foil about 5 inches long, and fold lengthwise 4 times to make long, strong strips about an inch wide. Put a strip around each end of the fish, fore and aft, and twist the ends to make tabs. Lay the oiled fish on a greased grill. Cook one side, then use the tabs to turn it over and, when it's done, to roll it onto a serving platter.

Fruity Fish Salad

Use tidbits of leftover fish or poach a pound of boneless fish to make this zesty salad. It's especially good with firm, meaty fish such as mahi mahi. Instead of the rice mix, you can substitute 3 cups leftover brown or white rice, adding your own herbs and spices to taste.

2 cups cold, cooked fish pieces
1 6-ounce package rice and
    wild rice mix, prepared
    according to package
    directions
1 cup celery, diced
1 cup red apple, diced

1 cup seedless grapes, halved
1 cup poppy-seed or butter-
    milk dressing
4 lettuce cups
raisins
slivered almonds

Toss fish, rice, celery, and fruit lightly with the dressing. Spoon into lettuce cups and sprinkle with raisins and almonds. Serves 4.

Serve with rolls or crackers and it's a complete meal.

Oyster Pudding

Cornbread and oysters are natural friends. Make a double batch of cornbread at breakfast time and save half for this one-dish dinner. Cook extra bacon at breakfast, too.

1 pound oysters, drained
juice of $1/2$ lemon
1 8-ounce can mushroom
    stems and pieces, drained
4 thick slices bacon, diced,
    cooked, and drained on
    paper towels
$1/2$ cup chopped sweet onion

$1/2$ cup chopped green pepper
$1/2$ cup chopped celery
1 clove garlic, minced
2 tablespoons butter
2 eggs
$3/4$ cup milk
about 2 cups cornbread, crum-
    bled

seafood

If the oysters are large, cut them into bite-size pieces and arrange in a buttered pan, casserole, or deep pie dish. Sprinkle with lemon juice, mushrooms, and bacon. Sauté vegetables in butter until crisp-tender, then sprinkle over oyster mixture. Beat eggs and milk and stir in the cornbread to make a chunky batter. Pour over the oyster mixture and bake at 350°F until set, about 35 minutes. Serves 4 to 6.

Lobster (or Crab) Sandwiches

One of my friends once gave me a recipe that called for "as many pecans as you can afford." That's the case with these sandwiches, in which a little lobster or crabmeat goes a long, flavorful way. They're best made with big, rich, buttery buns.

16 ounces finely shredded cabbage (or use prepackaged cabbage for coleslaw)	1 medium sweet onion, diced
	8 to 16 ounces (depending on your budget) cooked lobster
1 tablespoon sugar	or crabmeat
3/4 cup mayonnaise	8 to 10 hot-dog buns

Sprinkle cabbage with the sugar. Shred or finely chop the lobster or crabmeat. Toss everything together and pile into hot-dog buns. This is best if assembled just before serving. Makes 8 to 10 sandwiches.

It's easy to can surplus fish if you have jars and a pressure cooker. Ask your county home economist for directions, depending on the kinds of fish you angle for. In some parts of the country public canneries also cater to fishermen.

Individual Pizzas

This is another way to stretch a small catch, or to use bits of leftover cooked fish.

1 to 2 flour tortillas per person
oil
pizza sauce
sliced Bermuda onion
chunks of cooled, poached fish
thinly sliced avocado
grated Monterey Jack cheese

Fry each tortilla in a little oil until browned and puffy, and spread lightly with pizza sauce. Strew with onion, fish, avocado, and cheese. Bake in a 450°F oven just long enough to heat through and melt the cheese.

Although this takes some quick juggling in a small oven, baking time is fairly short so it works out if you set up an assembly line.

Fish in Foil

Have you noticed how important mustard has become in today's recipes? There are many types and flavors on the market. This is a good recipe for use with a classic Dijon mustard or, if you're more daring, one of the more exotic mustards such as raspberry, green peppercorn, or hazelnut.

4 fillets fresh fish
4 slices sweet onion
4 sprigs parsley, chopped
1 tablespoon fancy mustard
1 tablespoon lemon juice
$1/3$ cup mayonnaise
dash thyme

seafood

Set out 4 squares of nonstick foil and place a slice of onion on each. Sprinkle with chopped parsley, then add a piece of fish. Whisk mustard, lemon juice, and mayo together and pour over fish. Sprinkle lightly with thyme. Fold foil and bake atop a well-started grill about 10 minutes on each side, then test for doneness. Cook until fish flakes easily and is firm throughout. Serves 4.

While you're at it, grill corn on the cob and zucchini kebobs. Complete the meal with canned potato salad, muffins from the bakery, and popcorn balls for a dessert to munch on while taking a brisk walk.

Cioppino

There are as many recipes for this classic Mediterranean fish stew as there are Mediterranean cooks. If you carry canned clams, you'll be able to rustle up cioppino by catching or buying a good, firm, meaty fish. Buy canned clams with shells, and your cioppino will look authentic too.

$\frac{1}{3}$ cup olive oil	1 tablespoon Italian seasoning
1 large onion, diced	(basil and oregano)
1 green or red pepper, diced	2 to 2$\frac{1}{2}$ pounds fish fillets
1 teaspoon salt	10 ounces canned clams or 1
2 15- or 16-ounce cans tomatoes	dozen fresh clams
1 8-ounce can tomato sauce	fresh parsley
1 cup dry red wine	

Use your largest skillet or a roomy pot. Sauté onion and pepper in olive oil, then add garlic, tomatoes, tomato sauce, wine, and herbs. Bring to a boil, reduce heat, and simmer half an hour. Add fish in bite-size chunks, bring to a boil, arrange clams on top, and simmer just until fish is firm and clamshells open. Ladle into soup plates, arranging a clam or two on each serving, and sprinkle with chopped fresh parsley. Serves 8 to 10.

Put a crusty loaf of French or Italian bread on the table so each person can tear off pieces as desired to soak up the flavorful juices.

seafood

Make a batter for deep-fried fish by adding beer, ginger ale, lemon-lime soda, white wine diluted with water, or cola to pancake mix until it's like thick cream. Dip fish chunks in batter and drop them into sizzling fat.

Smoked Fish Casserole

Many RV travelers enjoy smoking their own fish. Or buy it as you go, experimenting with wonderful varieties—from smoked salmon in the Pacific Northwest to smoked kingfish and mullet in Florida. Then make this tangy, unusual, low-fat casserole.

1 pound smoked fish
8 ounces uncooked noodles
16 ounces creamy cottage cheese
1 clove garlic, minced
1 cup plain yogurt
1 small bunch scallions, sliced
grated Romano or Parmesan cheese

Skin, bone, and shred fish. Set aside. Cook and drain noodles. Combine everything except grated cheese and put in a buttered casserole. Sprinkle lightly with cheese and bake in a 350°F oven for about 25 minutes or until thoroughly heated. Serves 6.

Serve with rye rolls, carrot and celery sticks, and fresh fruit salad for dessert.

It's messy to dip fish in beaten eggs, then breadcrumbs. Instead, pat fish dry with paper towels and spread fillets with mayonnaise, then dip in seasoned crumbs or cornmeal you have spread on a paper plate.

Seafood Stew

In this stew, corn adds a sweetness to the seafood and crisp nuggets of salt pork lend a traditional touch. If you make it from canned fish, get as much variety as possible—tuna, crab, shrimp, salmon. Or use fresh fish. It's a quick, hearty warmer on a cold night.

8 ounces salt pork, diced
3 large onions, diced
1 pound boneless seafood, in chunks
1 14- to 16-ounce can cream-style corn
2 14- to 16-ounce cans potatoes, rinsed and drained (or 2 large potatoes, scrubbed and diced)

2 14- to 16-ounce cans tomatoes
1 10-ounce package frozen peas, thawed
salt, pepper
butter
thyme

In a big, heavy kettle, fry salt pork until crisp. Remove and drain on paper towels. Then sizzle onions in the fat until limp. Discard excess fat. Put seafood, corn, potatoes, and tomatoes (with their juice) into the pot and simmer gently about 30 minutes, stirring occasionally. Stir in peas, salt, and pepper just before serving. In each soup bowl place a pat of butter and sprinkle it with thyme, then ladle in the soup. Sprinkle with pork tidbits. Serves 4 to 6.

Serve with pilot crackers, a side dish of deli coleslaw, and saucer-size molasses cookies for dessert.

Seafood Pasta Primavera

The beauty of this recipe is that you can prepare the vegetables at home, ready to stir-fry the moment your ship comes in. The entire colorful, fresh meal throws together in one big skillet or wok. The pasta, too, can be cooked at home. Rinse it in cold water and drain it well, tossing it with 1 tablespoon of olive oil to keep it from sticking. Then pile it lightly (don't pack it down) into a container and keep cold until needed.

seafood

1 tablespoon peanut oil
1 large onion, diced
3 cloves garlic, minced
1 pound fresh asparagus, cut
   into $1/2$-inch slices
4 cups chopped fresh vegetables
   (mushrooms, broccoli and
   cauliflower florets, zucchini,
   bok choy)

2 tablespoons mixed Italian
   herbs
2 pounds fresh, boneless
   seafood in bite-size chunks
16 ounces linguine, cooked
   al dente
1 cup frozen peas, thawed
freshly grated Parmesan

Sizzle onion and garlic in hot oil in a large wok or skillet. Keeping heat high, add and stir-fry the other vegetables, herbs, and fish. Cook just until vegetables are crisp-tender and fish is cooked through. Lightly toss in pasta and peas and stir-fry until everything is heated through. Remove from heat. Sprinkle with cheese, toss again, and serve. Serves 6 to 8.

Just add a green salad and kaiser rolls slathered with butter, and you've made a banquet.

Crumb-Crusted Crab Casserole

Don't use artificial crabmeat or it won't be the same. Splurge on fresh lump crabmeat.

2 pounds crabmeat, picked
   over to remove any bits of
   shell
1 cup sour cream
$1/2$ teaspoon salt
1 tablespoon lemon juice
1 tablespoon finely chopped
   onion

$1/3$ cup grated Parmesan
   cheese
dash Tabasco sauce
$1/2$ stick butter, melted
about $3/4$ cup breadcrumbs
grated Parmesan cheese
   (optional)

Place crabmeat in a buttered casserole or 6 individual ramekins. Whisk together sour cream, salt, lemon juice, onion, and Tabasco, and spoon over crabmeat. Top with breadcrumbs, then drizzle butter over the top. Sprinkle with additional cheese if you like. Bake 20 minutes at 350°F. Serves 6.

If you assemble this ahead, keep it refrigerated several hours or overnight and add the breadcrumb topping just before baking. Baking time will be longer for a chilled casserole.

Make-Ahead Spaghetti in Clam Sauce

Assemble this casserole at home, and all you have to do is bake it until it's bubbly and fragrant.

16 ounces uncooked thin spaghetti
3 6-ounce cans chopped clams, with juice
$3/4$ cup extra virgin olive oil
8 cloves garlic, chopped
1 10- to 12-ounce bottle clam juice
2 teaspoons mixed Italian herbs
fresh chopped parsley
$1/3$ cup freshly grated Parmesan cheese

Cook spaghetti until barely tender and arrange in a buttered casserole. Sprinkle with chopped clams, reserving juice. In the same pot, heat olive oil and cook garlic until lightly browned. Add bottled clam juice to the reserved canned clam juice to make 3 cups, add it to garlic mixture, stir in parsley, and pour sauce over spaghetti. Cover with grated cheese and bake, uncovered, at 350°F until heated through, about 15 minutes. Serves 4.

If you want to assemble this at home, cover and keep refrigerated for up to two days. Add the grated cheese just before baking. Baking time will be about 30 to 35 minutes.

Complete the menu with baguettes of bread, a leafy salad, and coffee Galliano.

seafood

Leftover cooked fillets of fish? Roll out a tube of crescent rolls, seal perforations, and cut into 4 portions. Fold around 4 chunks of seasoned, cooked fish, moistening the edges to make a sealed package. Bake at 350°F for 25 minutes or until brown and puffy. Serve with tartar sauce.

Pan-Seared Tuna Steaks with Citrus Salsa

4 tuna steaks, fresh or
   thawed
1 tablespoon vegetable oil,
   preferably peanut

Marinade
1 tablespoon soy sauce
1 tablespoon olive oil
1 tablespoon lemon juice

Salsa
1 medium sweet onion (Vidalia,
   Texas Sweet), diced
1 rib celery, diced
1 10-ounce can mandarin
   oranges
1 15-ounce can grapefruit sections
2 tablespoons minced fresh
   cilantro
1 tablespoon olive oil
1 tablespoon lemon juice

Combine marinade ingredients, pour over tuna steaks, and marinate in the refrigerator for several hours. Meanwhile, make the salsa. Drain oranges and grapefruit, saving juices for another purpose. Toss fruit, vegetables, and cilantro with olive oil and lemon juice.

To cook, pan-sear steaks in peanut oil until crusty and caramelized on the outside and rare (or done to taste) inside. Spoon salsa over or beside the tuna steaks. Serves 4.

Salmon con Corn Salsa

Grill the salmon as described below, or use your favorite method. Then add a Mexicali touch with this salsa. It can be made ahead of time and chilled. When the cold salsa hits the hot salmon, flavors fly!

4 meaty salmon steaks
juice of 1 lime (reserve 1 tablespoon for salsa)
lemon pepper, cumin

Salsa
1 14- to 16-ounce can whole kernel corn, drained
1 medium red onion, diced
1 medium red pepper, diced
1 tablespoon lime juice
1 tablespoon olive oil
2 tablespoons minced fresh cilantro

Set out salmon steaks, sprinkle both sides with lime juice, lemon pepper, and cumin, and let stand 20 minutes. Broil or grill steaks 5 to 6 minutes per side or until done to your liking. Combine salsa ingredients in a small bowl and chill until ready to use. Serves 4.

Complete the meal with buttered corn sticks, sugar peas steamed with strips of sweet onion, and fresh mangoes for dessert.

Clamdigger Pie

1 6-ounce can chopped clams, drained
1 6-ounce can chunk salmon, drained
2 eggs, beaten
$2/3$ cup evaporated milk
1 10-ounce package frozen chopped spinach, thawed and drained
$1/4$ teaspoon nutmeg

Crust
2 cups instant mashed potatoes, prepared according to package directions
1 egg
1 tablespoon grated onion
2 tablespoons butter, melted

Mix seafood, eggs, milk, spinach, and seasonings and spread in a buttered baking dish or pan. To make crust, mix potatoes, onion, and egg. Spread over seafood mixture and drizzle with butter. Bake 25 minutes at 350°F. Let stand 5 minutes before serving. Serves 4.

Brown Rice Seafood Salad Supreme

This is another make-ahead summer salad that can be carried in the refrigerator for a quick lunch at a roadside rest stop when you're in a hurry to make a distant campsite before nightfall. Or serve it for dinner. It's filling and meaty yet very low in fat.

$1/2$ pound cooked shrimp,
    shelled and deveined
$1/2$ pound cooked bay scallops
2 cups cooked brown rice
$1/2$ cup julienned sweet pepper
$1/2$ cup frozen peas
$1/4$ cup sunflower seeds
$1/4$ cup raisins
1 cup julienned Jarlsberg
    cheese
greens for garnish

Dressing
1 cup plain yogurt
$1/2$ cup seeded and chopped
    cucumber
$1/2$ cup chopped green onion
1 tablespoon lemon juice
2 tablespoons soy sauce
dash pepper or lemon pepper

Combine dressing ingredients and set aside. Combine salad ingredients, add dressing, and chill. To serve, arrange greens on plates and spoon salad on them. Serves 4 to 6.

Serve with rye crispbread and sweet butter and, for dessert, thin slices of melon garnished with gjetost cheese (pronounced "YAY-tossed"). This tangy, caramel-colored cheese, served with plain crackers and a juicy fruit, makes a quick but chic dessert.

seafood

Surprise Ingredient Seafood Salad

Nobody will guess that this creamy salad contains an entire loaf of bread to stretch out a meager catch.

1 loaf day-old sandwich
   bread, crusts removed
   and cubed
4 hard-boiled eggs, diced
1 large sweet onion, minced

1 pound mixed, cooked seafood
   (shrimp, fish, crab, lobster,
   clams), in bite-size chunks
1 cup finely diced celery
2 cups light mayonnaise
1 cup nonfat plain yogurt

Pile bread cubes into a big mixing bowl. Add eggs, onion, seafood, celery, mayo, and yogurt and mix. Refrigerate overnight, stir, and you'll find that the bread has disappeared, creating a creamy and flavorful seafood salad. Makes about 6 cups.

Serve in lettuce cups or green pepper halves with lots of seasonal fresh vegetables and crisp crackers.

Ten

Some Like It in One Pot: One-Dish Meals

T hese recipes are made completely in one pan or casserole. Each is a complete meal to make and take from home or cook and serve in the RV. Although disposable foil containers can be used for casseroles, I don't recommend them for make-and-take recipes or for any food storage.

Garbanzo Bonanzo

This dish carries well and improves with reheating. Make it ahead at home and carry in a casserole to reheat in the microwave, or in boilable bags to heat atop the stove.

1 pound hot or sweet Italian
   sausage
1 large onion, diced
3 large cloves garlic, mashed
2 15- or 16-ounce cans stewed
   tomatoes
2 teaspoons mixed Italian herbs
2 cups water

16 ounces uncooked macaroni
1 16-ounce can garbanzo
   beans, drained
salt, pepper
minced fresh parsley
freshly grated Parmesan
   cheese

Cut sausages into small pieces and sizzle in a roomy pan with garlic and onion until sausages lose their pink color. Pour off any excess fat. Add tomatoes, herbs, and water and bring to a boil. Add macaroni and cook over high heat until tender. Reduce heat and add garbanzos. Heat thoroughly. Add salt and pepper to taste, stir in a handful of parsley, and sprinkle with cheese. Serves 6 to 8.

Serve in shallow soup plates with lots of garlic bread and a green salad with zesty Italian dressing.

Presto Pizza

Courtesy of Alaska Canned Salmon, the California Pistachio Commission, and Norseland Foods, this pizza throws together right in the pan in minutes. Look for pesto sauce in the refrigerated section of your supermarket with the fresh pastas and sauces. Or use your own favorite recipe.

1 tube refrigerated pizza dough (12-inch crust)
$^3/_4$ to 1 cup pesto sauce
1 cup coarsely chopped pistachios
1 7$^1/_2$-ounce can Alaska salmon, drained and flaked
3 cups grated Jarlsberg cheese

Arrange pizza dough in a 15-by-10-by-$^3/_4$-inch pan or a 12-inch pizza pan. Dot with pesto sauce. Sprinkle with pistachios and salmon and top with cheese. Bake at 425°F for 15 to 17 minutes or until crust is golden. Serves 4 to 6.

As a main dish, this goes well with a garnish of chilled cranberry sauce, soft breadsticks, and crunchy raw vegetables, followed by a tart, lemony dessert.

Fajizza Pizza

Don't forget to bring sour cream, tomatoes, guacamole, and shredded lettuce to serve with this Southwestern-style pizza.

1 prepared pizza crust	1 small red pepper, julienned
1 tablespoon olive oil	1 cup salsa (mild, medium, or
about 12 ounces chicken strips	hot)
(from boneless, skinless	8 ounces grated Monterey Jack
chicken breasts)	cheese
2 teaspoons chili powder	sour cream, diced tomatoes,
salt, pepper, garlic salt to taste	guacamole, shredded let-
1 large onion, diced	tuce
1 small green pepper, julienned	

Place pizza crust on baking sheet and brush with a little oil. Heat remaining oil in a nonstick skillet and stir-fry chicken strips with seasonings and vegetables until chicken is done through. Spread salsa on crust, top with chicken mixture, and sprinkle cheese over all. Bake at 425°F about 12 minutes, or until cheese is bubbly. Pass the toppings and dig in. Serves 4.

Pizza as You Like It

Keep on hand a supply of prebaked pizza crusts and vacuum-packed grated mozzarella cheese. Both are labeled with expiration dates but have fairly long shelf lives. Then use your imagination to create instant pizzas whenever you like. Simply bake any of these at 400°F until they're heated through and the mozzarella is bubbly. Suggested pizza toppings:

◆ A can of drained black beans tossed with half a packet of taco seasoning, chopped sweet onion, diced fresh tomatoes, and chopped parsley or cilantro. Spoon onto pizza base and top with mozzarella or jack cheese.

◆ Leftover vegetables such as broccoli or cauliflower florets and snipped green beans scattered atop a crust spread lightly with softened cream cheese. Sprinkle with dried basil and drizzle with pizza sauce. Top with mozzarella.

◆ Canned chunk chicken, sliced water chestnuts, and chunk pineapple, topped with mozzarella.

◆ Paper-thin slices of lox, tomato, and Bermuda onion arranged in overlapping profusion atop a crust spread with sour cream. Top with mozzarella.

◆ Sliced hard-boiled eggs sprinkled with crumbled, cooked bacon and grated mozzarella.

◆ A small can of corned beef, pulled apart, plus a 16-ounce can of sauerkraut, well drained. Top with mozzarella or grated Swiss cheese.

◆ Imitation crabmeat and canned Newburg sauce. Splash with sherry and top with mozzarella.

Chili Casserole

This is the simplest one-dish meal in the world. It's also colorful, complete, and will warm your jacket in the coldest autumn winds.

1 16-ounce can chili without beans	1 package Jiffy cornbread mix
1 16-ounce can kidney beans	1 egg
1 16-ounce can stewed tomatoes, Mexican style	water
1 11-ounce can Mexicorn (reserve liquid)	grated jack cheese (optional)
	Tabasco (optional)

Dump chili, beans, and tomatoes into a roomy saucepan and heat. Meanwhile, empty cornbread mix into a plastic bag and add liquid from the Mexicorn, about half the corn, the egg, and enough water to make a thick batter. Blend only until evenly moistened. Stir remaining corn into chili. When chili mixture comes to a boil, drizzle batter over it, cover, lower heat, and simmer just until cornbread is set. Ladle into bowls and pass the grated cheese and Tabasco. Serves 6.

Serve with crunchy celery sticks and plan a quenching dessert such as sorbet.

one-dish meals

Cock-a-Leekie Casserole

4 large, skinless chicken thighs
2 tablespoons oil
2 leeks
2 cups water
2 chicken bouillon cubes
2 tablespoons instant-blend flour
1 cup pitted prunes, cut up
salt, pepper to taste

Brown chicken in oil and drain excess fat. Cut up and add the white portion of the leeks, plus the water and bouillon cubes. Cover and simmer until meat is very tender, then add prunes. Make a paste with the flour and a little water, stir into chicken mixture, bring to a boil, then season to taste. Serve in bowls or soup plates. Serves 4.

Serve with slabs of French bread to soak up the gravy. Add a side salad of mixed greens, sliced radishes, and grated carrots with a poppy-seed dressing, and a colorful dessert such as baked apples sauced with cherry yogurt.

Brunswick Stew

Let this simmer on the galley stove all afternoon on a chilly day or use a pressure cooker to speed cooking. The meat must fall apart into shreds. This makes a big batch that is great for campground potluck suppers. Or cook it by the gallon at home to freeze for future campouts.

2 pounds skinless chicken
    thighs
2 pounds lean chuck
2 pounds lean pork
8 cups water
3 large onions, diced
1 46-ounce can tomato juice
4 16-ounce cans cream-style
    corn

1 16-ounce can green lima
    beans
3 tablespoons vinegar
1 tablespoon dried sage
salt, pepper
hot sauce to taste

Choose very lean beef and pork roasts and have the butcher grind them coarsely. Bring meats, water, and onion to a boil in a large, heavy kettle over a high flame. Reduce heat, cover, and simmer until meats are very tender. Remove thighs, discard bones, and chop meat. Return chicken to stew with remaining ingredients, and cook over medium heat, stirring often to prevent scorching, until well heated. Serves 20 to 24.

Serve in soup bowls with a hearty whole-wheat bread, apple butter, raw vegetable sticks, and gingerbread with vanilla sauce for dessert.

Cassoulet

1 pound sweet Italian sausage
3 pounds lamb for stew
3 15- or 16-ounce cans great
    northern or other white beans
1 pound carrots, chopped
4 ribs celery, sliced

2 large onions, diced
1 15- or 16-ounce can beef
    broth
2 tablespoons instant-blend
    flour
salt, pepper, thyme

Cut sausage into chunks. In a big Dutch oven, fry sausage and lamb over high heat until browned. Pour off excess fat. Add vegetables and broth, cover, and simmer over a low-medium flame until lamb is tender. Make a paste with the flour and a little water and add to pot. Boil to thicken somewhat; thin with water or red wine if necessary to make a soupy stew. Season to taste. Serve in soup plates, with lots of French bread. Serves 8 to 12.

Put leftovers in a boilable bag to reheat without having to wash a pot.

one-dish meals

Lamb Shanks

4 lamb shanks
flour mixed with salt and pepper
2 to 3 tablespoons oil
2 large onions, diced
$1/4$ teaspoon cinnamon
8 dried apricot halves

8 pitted prunes
1 16-ounce can potatoes, rinsed and drained
1 16-ounce can whole baby carrots, drained

Trim any excess fat from lamb shanks and dredge in seasoned flour and brown in oil. Cover with water, bring to a boil, cover, and simmer until the lamb is almost tender. Add onions, cinnamon, apricots, and prunes and simmer until everything is tender, adding more water if necessary. Add potatoes and carrots and heat through. Serves 4.

Serve with a lime Jell-O salad, a rich challah loaf, and a dessert of Popsicles to take on an after-dinner stroll.

Ham and Broccoli Bake

2 10-ounce packages frozen chopped broccoli, thawed
1 pound canned ham, diced
6 ounces grated sharp cheddar cheese
3 cups milk
4 eggs
2 cups biscuit mix
$1/2$ teaspoon thyme

Spread broccoli in a buttered 13-by-9-inch casserole. Top with ham and cheese and put in a 350°F oven. Beat milk and eggs together, then beat in biscuit mix just until evenly moistened. Remove casserole from oven, pour on batter, and drift with thyme. Return to oven and bake for about 50 minutes, or until the crust is golden brown. Serves 6 to 8.

One-Step Casserole

This is one to use with the meat, onion, and green pepper mixture described on page 95. Many RVers cook big batches of this ahead of time at home and freeze it in meal-size portions for camping trips. This mixture is the basis for many family favorites, including chili and spaghetti sauce. Traditionalists prefer lean ground beef, sometimes with some ground veal and ground pork added, but you can also use all or part ground turkey.

2$\frac{1}{2}$ cups cooked meat mixture
salt, pepper
1 15-ounce can tomato sauce
1 28- to 32-ounce can tomatoes
1$\frac{1}{2}$ cups water
8 ounces uncooked wide noodles
8 ounces grated cheddar or Monterey Jack cheese

Sprinkle uncooked noodles in a baking pan and top with meat mixture, seasonings, tomato sauce, tomatoes, and water. Cover with foil and bake for 45 minutes at 350°F. Remove from oven, take off foil, add cheese, and bake a few minutes more until cheese melts. Let stand 10 minutes and serve with Italian bread and a leafy salad. Serves 4 to 5.

one-dish meals

First Night in Camp Casserole

Assemble this all-in-one meal at home and carry it in the refrigerator. While you travel, flavors blend and the macaroni "cooks" itself.

2 cups milk
2 cans condensed cream of
    mushroom soup
8 ounces uncooked macaroni
1 6$^{1}/_{2}$-ounce can water
    chestnuts
2 6$^{1}/_{2}$-ounce cans chunk
    chicken

6 ounces grated cheddar
1 medium onion, finely
    chopped
$^{1}/_{2}$ green pepper, diced
handful fresh parsley, minced

one-dish meals

Whisk together milk and soup to make a smooth sauce. Arrange remaining ingredients evenly in a buttered 3-quart bake-and-serve casserole and cover with milk mixture. Cover and refrigerate for at least 8 hours. Bake covered casserole at 350°F for about 75 minutes, remove from oven, and let stand 10 minutes. Serves 6.

If you've brought split and buttered rolls, a bag of washed and cut-up celery and carrot sticks, and a bag of Tootsie Pops for dessert, your first night's meal is complete.

Pasta Fazuli

Although there are countless versions and various spellings of this filling favorite, this is one of the many "right" ways to prepare a versatile one-dish classic. Make it two to three days ahead and warm up aboard, or throw it together in the galley in minutes.

1 pound sweet Italian sausage
1 large onion, diced
2 to 3 ribs celery, diced
3 cloves garlic, minced
1 16-ounce can chicken broth
1 16-ounce can great northern
    beans

1$^{1}/_{2}$ cups water
1 cup uncooked macaroni
$^{1}/_{2}$ cup freshly grated Romano
    cheese
salt (optional)

If sausage is in casings, remove them. Break up and brown sausage in a large skillet with vegetables. Drain excess fat. Add chicken broth, water, and beans with their liquid. Bring to a boil, add macaroni, cover, and simmer over very low flame until macaroni is tender and moisture is absorbed. Add salt to taste. Fold in cheese just before serving or sprinkle atop each serving. Serves 4.

Add a green salad with Italian dressing and an Italian loaf, thickly sliced, to make a banquet.

Chili Under a Blanket

Get out your largest kettle, preferably one that can go directly from stove to table. A large skillet or Dutch oven is best, because it's large enough in diameter to accommodate the dozen biscuits that form the warm blanket that turns this into a one-dish feast.

3 pounds ground turkey	2 tablespoons mixed Italian
3 large onions, diced	herbs
3 tablespoons minced garlic	1 tablespoon cumin
2 large carrots, diced	1 20-ounce can kidney beans
2 green peppers, diced	salt, pepper (optional)
2 jalapeño peppers, seeded	2 to 3 dashes hot sauce
and diced	
1 15-ounce can tomato sauce	*Biscuit Topping*
1½ cups water	3 cups biscuit mix
2 beef bouillon cubes (or 2	16 ounces plain yogurt
teaspoons bouillon granules)	12 ounces grated jack cheese
2 tablespoons sweet paprika	

Brown turkey, using a little oil if necessary, with onions and garlic. Add remaining ingredients, cover, and simmer until everything is tender and flavorful.

Meanwhile, mix biscuit mix and yogurt, adding a little extra milk if necessary, to make a thick dough. Fold in cheese and turn out onto a floured dishtowel. Knead briefly, just to blend well. Pat dough into a circle about ½ inch thick, and cut into quarters, then thirds, to form 12 wedges. Bake at 425°F on a lightly greased baking sheet for 15 minutes, or until golden brown. Arrange biscuits atop the hot chili. Serves 12.

Complete the meal with individual dishes of a firefighting salad such as lime Jell-O with grated carrots. For dessert, haul the watermelon out of the creek where it's been cooling and serve big, juicy wedges.

Jumble YaYa

1 cup diced ham
1 large onion, diced
1 medium green pepper, diced
1 rib celery, diced
2 to 3 cooked breakfast
   sausage links, cut up
1 cup uncooked long-grain rice
1 $\frac{1}{2}$ cups water (use part bottled
   clam juice if you like)

$\frac{1}{2}$ teaspoon thyme
1 pound shelled, deveined
   shrimp
1 cup frozen peas, thawed
salt, pepper to taste
Tabasco to taste

In a roomy kettle, sizzle ham, onion, pepper, and sausage, adding a little oil if necessary. Pour off any excess fat. Stir in rice, then add water, thyme, and Tabasco (if desired). Bring to a boil, cover, and cook over low heat until rice is tender, about 20 minutes. Turn up heat and add shrimp, stirring lightly to keep from burning. Cook until shrimp are firm and pink. Stir in peas and heat through, then adjust seasonings. Serves 4.

Serve with toasted garlic bread and gallons of green salad. For dessert, pass out individual bags of jellybeans, in each person's favorite flavor or color, to munch while you play a twilight game of Frisbee.

one-dish meals

Pizza Puff

If you're using the meat, onion, and green pepper mixture made in advance at home (see page 95), substitute 3 cups of it for the ground meat, onion, garlic, and green pepper listed below, and put it directly into the baking dish. Stir in the spaghetti sauce mix, tomato sauce, and water and proceed.

1 pound ground beef or turkey	8 ounces grated mozzarella
1 large onion, diced	cheese
2 cloves garlic, minced	2 eggs
1 green pepper, diced	1 cup milk
1 1-ounce packet spaghetti	1 cup flour
sauce seasoning mix	about $1/2$ cup freshly grated
1 15-ounce can tomato sauce	Parmesan cheese
$1/2$ cup water	

Brown meat and vegetables in a pan that can go from stove top to oven to table. Pour off excess fat and add spaghetti sauce mix, tomato sauce, and water. Sprinkle with mozzarella. Whisk together eggs, milk, and flour and pour over the dish, then sprinkle with Parmesan and bake at 400°F for about 30 minutes or until golden brown. The batter will puff up around the meat, forming its own crust. Whisk it to the table before the puff collapses and cut and serve at once. Serves 6 to 8.

Stovetop Rice Pizza

For this you'll need a roomy, nonstick, 12-inch skillet. It's a way to make wheat-free pizza, and it uses up leftover rice.

3 cups cooked rice
2 eggs, beaten
1 6-ounce jar sliced mushrooms
pepperoni as desired
1 8-ounce can tomato sauce
1 teaspoon mixed Italian herbs
other toppings, ad lib
6 ounces grated mozzarella cheese

Stir eggs into rice and press around bottom and sides of a cold, lightly greased, nonstick skillet to form a crust. Cover and cook over medium flame until eggs begin to set. Top with mushrooms, pepperoni, any other favorite toppings, then drizzle with tomato sauce. Sprinkle with Italian herbs, then with cheese. Cover and continue cooking over low-medium flame until cheese is melted and crust is set. Let stand a few minutes for easier cutting. Serves 4.

To serve from the pan, use a nonmetal cutter that won't damage the nonstick finish. Divide into wedges and serve on plates with a mound of salad and sesame breadsticks.

one-dish meals

Eleven

One Potato, Two: Starches and Side Dishes

If you're like many RV campers, you make many a meal out of meat from the grill, a starch side dish, and a big salad. With a broiled chop or burger these recipes are basic meal makers.

Bread Salad #1

This is not only a quick and easy starch side dish to serve with a plain meat, it's a good way to use stale bread on those trips when you've brought too much.

> 1 loaf stale French bread, cut into ½-inch cubes
> 2 firm, ripe tomatoes, diced
> ¼ cup sunflower seeds
> 1 small sweet onion, diced
> 1 tablespoon minced fresh parsley
> Italian dressing to taste

Let bread cubes air dry. Toss with rest of ingredients and serve at once. If you don't have fresh parsley, use a sprinkling of dill; dried parsley doesn't have enough zest for this dish. Serves 4 to 6.

Sauerkraut Noodle Skillet

This recipe was developed by the National Kraut Packers Association. It's a tangy side dish to serve with grilled pork chops or baked ham, but it's robust enough to serve as a main dish for a light supper. If you make it ahead at home to warm up in the microwave, the flavor will be better developed.

1 tablespoon vegetable oil	1 teaspoon caraway seeds
1 medium onion, sliced	1 cup chicken broth
1 1/2 cups sliced mushrooms	1 cup plain yogurt
2 cups sauerkraut, rinsed and drained	1/2 cup part-skim ricotta cheese
1 tablespoon sweet paprika	6 ounces uncooked medium egg noodles
2 teaspoons flour	

Sauté onion and mushrooms in oil in a large skillet. Stir in sauerkraut. Sprinkle flour, paprika, and caraway seeds over mixture, then stir in broth and simmer 25 minutes. Whisk ricotta and yogurt together and add to sauerkraut mixture. Heat but do not boil. Cook and drain noodles, then toss with sauerkraut mixture. Serves 6.

Savory Rice Salad

On a hot night have this ready in the refrigerator to serve with any meat from the campsite's barbecue grill. It serves as a starch and salad in one. Add a bouquet of grilled vegetables to complete the plate.

2 cups uncooked instant rice	2 tablespoons sliced scallions
2 cups boiling water	1 cup additional vegetables as desired (diced celery, grated carrots, thawed peas)
2 tablespoons white wine vinegar	
1 tablespoon olive oil	1 cup chopped tomato
1/4 teaspoon salt	1/3 cup sliced olives
1/4 teaspoon sugar	
1/4 teaspoon pepper	

starches and side dishes

Place rice in a heatproof bowl. Pour water over rice, cover, and let stand 5 minutes or until rice is tender. Stir vinegar, oil, salt, sugar, and pepper together and pour over rice. Stir to mix completely, then mix in vegetables. Serve at room temperature or chill until serving time. Serves 4 to 6.

Pasta à la Grecque

The word orzo *means barley yet, like other pastas, it's made from wheat. Because of its small size and ricelike shape, it's easy to toast first in butter, giving it a rich and nutty taste.*

2 tablespoons butter
1 tablespoon minced garlic
1 $\frac{1}{2}$ cups uncooked orzo
1 1-ounce packet onion-mushroom soup mix
3 $\frac{1}{4}$ cups water
6 ounces mushrooms, sliced
2 to 3 scallions, thinly sliced

In a 3-quart saucepan melt butter over medium-high heat. Add garlic and orzo and cook until golden, stirring constantly. Stir in soup mix and water. Bring to a boil, cover, and simmer 10 minutes. Add mushrooms but do not stir. Cover and simmer 10 minutes more over very low flame. Turn off heat and let stand 10 to 15 minutes to absorb remaining liquid. Fluff with a fork, scatter with scallions, and serve. Serves 6 to 8 as a side dish or 3 to 4 as a main dish.

Boil quartered red potatoes just until tender and marinate in a vinaigrette dressing overnight, adding chunks of cucumbers, celery, sweet pepper, and other raw vegetables if you like. Thread on skewers and serve as a cold potato salad-on-a-stick.

starches and side dishes

Green Rice Casserole

Anytime you can combine a starch and a vegetable or two in a rich, creamy, colorful casserole, you save time and dishwashing. This casserole goes well with grilled chicken, or it can stand alone as a vegetarian main dish. Assemble the casserole at home and keep it cold to nuke on the first night out.

2 cups uncooked instant rice
2 cups boiling water
2 tablespoons butter
1 10-ounce package frozen
    chopped broccoli, thawed
    and drained
1 small onion, diced
3 tablespoons instant-blend flour

1 teaspoon prepared mustard
1 1/2 cups milk
4 ounces grated cheddar
    cheese
1/3 cup seasoned breadcrumbs
bits of butter

Place rice in a lightly greased casserole (or use nonstick spray), add boiling water, cover tightly, and let stand 5 minutes or until rice is tender. In a nonstick skillet, melt butter and sauté broccoli and onion until crisp-tender. Stir in flour and mustard, then continue stirring over low flame while adding milk. Fold vegetable mixture and cheese into rice. Top with breadcrumbs and dot with butter. Bake uncovered at 350°F until heated through. Serves 6 as a side dish or 4 as a main dish.

Oven Fries

2 large baking potatoes
1 egg white
1/2 cup grated Parmesan cheese
2 teaspoons oregano

Scrub potatoes and cut each lengthwise into 8 wedges. Combine cheese and oregano. Beat egg white until foamy. Dip potatoes in egg white, then in cheese mixture. Bake on a well-greased baking sheet at 425°F for 25 minutes, or until golden outside and tender inside. Serves 4.

Mashed Potato Pie

One of the shortcuts I use in RV cooking is instant mashed potatoes but, to be honest, they need a little help before they can pass muster. Here's one way to disguise them. The result is twice-baked potatoes in a flaky crust.

1 deep-dish pie crust
6 servings instant mashed potatoes
2 eggs, beaten
$1/3$ cup grated Parmesan cheese
$1/2$ cup yogurt or sour cream

Prick pie crust all over with a fork and bake at 450°F for 5 minutes, then set aside. Prepare potatoes according to package directions, then stir in remaining ingredients and spread on pie crust. Bake at 425°F until crust is brown and filling is set, about 30 to 40 minutes. Let stand 5 minutes, then serve in wedges. Serves 6 to 8.

Wild Rice Stovetop Dressing

1 6-ounce box rice and wild rice mix
2 tablespoons butter
$1^{1}/2$ cups water
1 cup orange juice
1 tablespoon fresh orange zest
$1/2$ cup toasted pecans

Sauté rice in butter until brown, then stir in seasoning packet, water, orange juice, and orange zest. Bring to a boil, cover, reduce heat, and simmer until liquid is absorbed, about 25 minutes. Stir in pecans just before serving. Serves 6.

This is good with chicken or pork. You can buy roasted, salted pecans or toast your own in a hot, dry skillet.

starches and side dishes

Confetti Risotto

Use lots of colorful vegetables with rice to make an appealing side dish that has starch and vegetables all in one.

1 10-ounce package frozen chopped spinach, thawed and drained
1 14- or 15-ounce can chicken broth plus water
3 tablespoons butter
1 1/2 cups uncooked arborio rice
1 tablespoon minced garlic
1 cup diced onion
1/4 teaspoon hot sauce
2 teaspoons dried oregano
1/3 cup grated Parmesan
1 small carrot, thinly sliced
1 rib celery, thinly sliced

Press out excess moisture from spinach. Add enough water to chicken broth to make 2 1/2 cups of liquid. Combine hot sauce, oregano, and cheese and set aside. Melt butter in a roomy saucepan and sauté the rice, garlic, and onion. Gradually stir in broth mixture, add the carrot and celery, bring to a boil, cover, reduce heat, and simmer 20 minutes. Turn off heat. Stir in cheese and spice mixture, cover again, and let stand 5 minutes. Serves 6.

For added color, stir in a handful of thawed green peas when you add the cheese and spices.

Oven-Broasted Potatoes

Although it calls for only three ingredients, this recipe is an entire symphony of meaty, crusty flavors. It goes especially well with steak or hamburgers from the outdoor grill.

2 pounds small red potatoes, scrubbed and quartered
1 4-serving packet Lipton onion soup mix
1/3 cup virgin olive oil

Put potatoes in a zip-top plastic bag and add soup mix and oil. Zip bag closed and toss until potatoes are well coated. Turn out onto a lightly oiled, shallow cooking pan or casserole and bake at 450°F, stirring occasionally, 40 minutes or until crispy on the outside and tender inside. Serves 6 to 8.

starches and side dishes

Potatoes Fan-Tastic

6 Idaho potatoes, peeled
1 teaspoon chicken bouillon granules
$^3/_4$ cup water
$^1/_2$ stick butter
freshly ground pepper
$^1/_3$ cup breadcrumbs
3 tablespoons freshly grated Parmesan

Cut potatoes into thin slices without cutting all the way through so slices will fan out slightly. Stir bouillon granules into water. Place potatoes in a greased, shallow baking pan and pour chicken bouillon over them. Melt butter and pour about half of it over potatoes. Bake 30 minutes at 375°F, then sprinkle with breadcrumbs and drizzle with remaining butter. Bake another 10 to 15 minutes or until potatoes are tender, then sprinkle with grated cheese and serve. Serves 6.

Garlicky Grits

If you haven't yet discovered grits as an alternative to potatoes, now is the time.

1 cup uncooked regular grits
1 stick butter
6 ounces grated cheddar
2 cloves garlic, minced
2 eggs
milk

Cook grits according to package directions. When done, turn off heat and stir in butter, garlic, and cheese. Cover and set aside to cool a bit. Break eggs into a measuring cup, then add enough milk to make 1 cup. Beat eggs and milk, then stir into grits. Turn into a greased casserole. At this point, refrigerate to bake later, if desired. To continue, bake 45 minutes at 350°F. Serves 6.

starches and side dishes

Dressed-Up Squash

This casserole freezes well, so make up a large supply at home and freeze it in batches sized for your family. It's the perfect accompaniment for a meal from the grill.

3 pounds yellow squash
1 can condensed cream of
 chicken soup
8 ounces regular or low-fat sour
 cream
1 medium onion, diced, or
 several scallions, thinly sliced

4 ounces grated cheddar
 cheese
1 stick butter (no substitutes),
 melted
1 8-ounce package Pepperidge
 Farm Herb Seasoned Stuffing

Boil squash just until crisp-tender. Whisk together soup and sour cream and mix lightly with squash, onion, and cheese. Place in a sprayed casserole. Toss stuffing with butter. Mix half into squash mixture and place the rest on top. At this point, cover and freeze, if desired. To continue, thaw casserole if frozen, then cover and bake 30 minutes at 350°F. Remove cover and bake 5 to 10 minutes more or until crusty brown. Serves 6 to 8.

starches and side dishes

Shamrock Rice

2 cups hot instant rice, prepared according to package directions
$1/2$ cup minced fresh parsley (no substitutes)
3 scallions, including some green part, thinly sliced
grated zest of 1 lime
salt to taste

Fold parsley, scallions, and lime zest lightly into rice, salt to taste, and serve with fish or chicken. Serves 5 or 6.

Bring a big pot of water to a boil and cook, in the same water, noodles plus boil-in-the-bag creamed spinach. Drain the noodles and stir in the spinach with a nugget of butter and a hefty dose of grated Romano.

Saffron Rice

There is no substitute for saffron, which is very expensive but worth the splurge when you want a special rice dish to accompany that once-in-a-life-time catch of fresh salmon or walleye.

1 medium onion, diced
1 stick butter
1 1/4 cups uncooked long-grain rice
1/4 cup white wine or white grape juice
1/4 tablespoon saffron threads
about 1 cup sliced mushrooms
2 cups water
2 teaspoons chicken bouillon granules
1/3 cup frozen green peas, thawed

Sauté onion in some of the butter until translucent, then add rice and remaining butter and stir until rice also looks translucent. Stir in mushrooms. Add wine and bring to a boil. Add water, bouillon, and saffron and return to a boil. Cover and simmer over very low heat, or bake in a covered casserole at 350°F, for 20 minutes or until water is absorbed and rice is tender. Stir in peas and serve. Serves 6.

Calypso Beans 'n' Rice

Almost every island in the Caribbean has its own version of beans and rice. The only variation is the type of bean and the degree of hotness. For the beans use black (turtle) beans, kidney beans, pigeon peas, pinto beans, or red beans. Navy beans or limas are not traditional.

starches and side dishes

1 16-ounce can beans, drained
3 cups water
1 16-ounce can coconut milk (not cream of coconut)
2 cups uncooked rice
2 teaspoons minced garlic
$^1/_2$ teaspoon dried thyme
1 tablespoon tomato paste (optional)
salt, pepper, hot sauce to taste

What could be easier? Simply combine everything in a roomy, heavy, lidded pot, bring to a boil, reduce heat, and simmer without stirring until all the liquid is absorbed. With regular, long-grain rice this takes 20 to 25 minutes. Stir and serve, with additional hot sauce on the side if you like. Serves 8 to 10 as a side dish or 4 to 6 as a main dish.

Yorkshire Pudding

It's really just a great big popover. The ingredients whisk together in seconds, yet this puffs up to make an impressive pancake that everybody loves. In England it's made right in the meat drippings, but by using butter you can make it anytime to serve with any meat.

3 tablespoons butter
1 cup flour
1 cup milk
1 teaspoon salt
2 eggs

Heat oven to 400°F and melt butter in a 10-inch round pie plate or an 8-by-10-inch casserole. Swirl butter to coat the bottom and sides thoroughly. Whisk flour, milk, salt, and eggs together just until smooth and pour onto butter. Bake 30 minutes or until golden and puffy, then race it to the table before it collapses. Serves 4 to 6.

starches and side dishes

Stuffing Stuffed Tomatoes

When tomatoes are ripe and seasonal, buy them by the bushel along the roadside and splurge on this colorful side dish with any meat.

tomatoes
stovetop-style stuffing

Slice off tops of meaty, ripe tomatoes and scoop out insides. Discard seeds and watery pulp. If necessary, take a tiny slice off the bottom of each tomato so they will stand up in a baking pan. Now stir up some top-of-the-stove stuffing according to package directions, or use your own recipe, and pile it loosely in the tomato shells. Bake at 350°F for 15 to 20 minutes or until heated through and brown on top. Plan 1 tomato per person, with a few extras for hefty eaters.

Variations: Try this with any type of stuffing—rice, cornbread, wild rice, or even your favorite oyster stuffing.

Baked Bulgur

Once you discover the ease of cooking with bulgur, which is an ancient version of precooked "fast" food, you'll want to try it in many recipes or as a hot breakfast cereal.

3 tablespoons butter
1 cup bulgur (parboiled whole wheat)
1 medium onion, diced
2 to 3 ribs celery, diced
2 cups water
2 teaspoons chicken bouillon granules

Melt butter in a heavy saucepan and sauté bulgur with vegetables. Add water and bouillon, bring to a boil, cover, reduce heat, and simmer 15 minutes. Remove pan from heat and let stand a few minutes, then fluff with a fork and serve. Serves 6 to 8.

Tabbouleh

Tabbouleh is a Middle Eastern starch dish that utilizes bulgur without cooking. It's best if made ahead and chilled thoroughly.

1 cup bulgur
1 cup boiling water
1 clove garlic
several scallions, finely sliced
1 cup freshly chopped parsley
1 2¼-ounce can sliced ripe olives, drained

2 tomatoes, seeded and diced
¼ cup virgin olive oil
⅓ cup lemon juice
1 teaspoon salt
½ teaspoon mixed Italian herbs

Place bulgur and garlic in a large bowl, stir in water, cover, and let stand for 30 minutes. Discard garlic. Fold in remaining vegetables. Whisk olive oil and lemon juice together with salt and herbs and toss with bulgur mixture. Cover and chill. Serve with cold cuts, meat hot from the grill, or a roast. Serves 6 to 8.

Variation: To make this a hearty, main-dish salad, fold in a can of well-drained garbanzo beans.

Hash Brown Hustle

1 2-pound package frozen hash browns, thawed
1 small onion, finely diced
1 can condensed cream of celery soup
16 ounces sour cream
10 ounces grated cheddar
½ stick butter, melted
1½ cups cornflake crumbs

Butter a 3-quart casserole. Mix together everything but melted butter and cornflake crumbs and pile into the casserole. Sprinkle with a generous layer of crumbs and drizzle with butter. Bake 1 hour at 350°F. Serves 8.

For messless mixing, smoosh everything (except the butter and crumbs) together in an extra-large food storage bag and strip it out into the casserole. Then just throw the bag away.

starches and side dishes

___

Barbecued Potatoes

butter
onions
potatoes
barbecue sauce

Layer sliced onions and potatoes in a heavily buttered casserole, using 1 onion for each 2 potatoes (plan on 1 medium potato per person). Drizzle each layer lightly with your favorite barbecue sauce. Cover and bake at 350°F for 45 minutes or until vegetables are tender. Then uncover, add more barbecue sauce, and bake 15 minutes more.

Variation: Try making this on the grill, in a heavy-duty foil bag over medium coals. Turn every 10 minutes and test for doneness after 30 minutes.

Fast Lane

◆ Make your own prepackaged rice pilaf mix at home. Into each zip-top plastic bag put ingredients for one batch. They include rice, chicken or beef bouillon granules, raisins, curry powder, and dried onion flakes.

◆ Experiment with different rices, not just white and brown but long and short grain, arborio, and aromatic. Each produces a different result, giving simple meals more variety.

◆ Dress up deli potato salad by adding caraway seeds, sliced scallions, sliced radishes, diced sweet pepper, diced tomato, sliced stuffed olives, or a seeded, diced cucumber.

◆ Stuck for a quick starch dish? For each portion, empty a single-serving pouch of plain or flavored instant grits into a ramekin. Stir in boiling water and top with a pat of butter.

◆ To make a serving of sticky rice look more festive, serve it with an ice-cream scoop.

Twelve

Light My Fire!

M any RV travelers have fond memories of their campfire days and still make the occasional meal in a Dutch oven, while almost everyone grills outdoors at least some of the time. These recipes are for outdoor cooking on a campfire, open grill, or covered grill. Some fine-tuning may have to be done according to your cooking fuel and the type of grill, but these ideas are all time-savers, delicious, and RV doable.

For slow-cooking in the oven, use any ovenproof casserole with a tight lid, such as Pyrex or Chantal. For campfire baking I prefer a Dutch oven that is cast aluminum. It heats more evenly than cast iron and is lighter to carry. For all-day campfire cooking, you may need a separate feeder fire so you can add fresh, hot coals every few hours. Don't peek under the lid too often since that allows heat and steam to escape. Dutch oven cooking, whether it's done in the campfire or oven or on the stove top, relies on an even, undisturbed envelope of heat and moisture.

Corned Beef in Beer

4 to 5 onions, sliced
1 12-ounce bottle or can beer
1 4- or 5-pound round of corned beef, well trimmed of fat

Layer onions in the bottom of a Dutch oven. Add corned beef and beer. Cover and bake 8 to 10 hours at 225°F or bury in well-started coals all day. When you get back from the ATV trails, fishing, or the beach, remove the corned beef to a cutting board and slice across the grain. Top with the onion-beer sauce. Serves 10 to 12.

Serve with slabs of rye bread, sweet butter, and big dill pickles. If you want additional vegetables, boil a big pot of scrubbed potatoes and peeled carrots atop the stove (or cook in the microwave), sprinkle with caraway seeds, and serve swimming in butter.

Barbecued Ribs

This recipe is courtesy of West Bend. I've adapted it for Dutch oven cookery.

4 pounds lean country-style pork ribs
1 can condensed tomato soup
$\frac{1}{2}$ cup cider vinegar
$\frac{1}{2}$ cup brown sugar, firmly packed
1 tablespoon soy sauce
1 teaspoon celery seed
1 teaspoon chili powder

Trim excess fat from ribs, cut into 3- or 4-rib portions, and place in Dutch oven. Combine remaining ingredients and pour over ribs. Cover and bake 6 to 8 hours at 225°F, 4 hours at 275°F, or bury in a bed of well-started coals all day. Serves 4.

This is a meal for paper plates and fingers. Eat it with chunks of Italian bread to mop up the sauce, coleslaw, grilled corn on the cob, and spears of fresh pineapple, followed by generous portions of premoistened towelettes.

campfire cooking

Stuffed Cabbage

Make the cabbage rolls a day or two ahead of time at home and carry in the refrigerator in a tightly lidded plastic container. Add the tomatoes just before cooking.

1 large cabbage
1 pound lean ground beef
1 teaspoon salt
$^1/_2$ teaspoon pepper
$^2/_3$ cup uncooked white rice
1 small onion, chopped
1 16-ounce can tomatoes
1 8-ounce can tomato sauce

Core cabbage and place it, cored side down, in a few inches of boiling water for a few minutes to wilt leaves. Remove 8 outer leaves and coarsely chop remaining cabbage. Mix ground beef, salt, pepper, rice, and onion. Divide meat mixture among the cabbage leaves and roll up. Cover and refrigerate. To proceed, put remaining chopped cabbage in the bottom of a Dutch oven. Top with cabbage rolls, seam side down. Pour on the tomatoes and tomato sauce. Bake 1 hour at 325°F or bury in well-started coals all day. Serves 4.

Complete the meal with rich egg-braid bread, a leafy salad, and apple tarts.

Finnish Stew

This is a sort of Scandinavian beef bourguignonne, fork-tender and steeped in mysterious flavors. The secret is to use three different meats and lots of onions. With various combinations, the flavor is subtly different.

4 pounds boneless cubed meat (beef, turkey, lamb, pork, veal)
6 medium onions, sliced
2 teaspoons whole allspice
1 tablespoon salt

campfire cooking

Combine all ingredients in a Dutch oven. Cook 6 to 7 hours in a conventional or convection oven at 250°F or bury in well-started coals all day. Serves 8 to 10.

Serve with boiled new potatoes in dill and butter, rye bread, and a medley of root vegetables. For dessert, serve fresh or canned fruit with Danish butter cookies.

Mexican Stew

3 pounds turkey or pork (or some of each), cubed
1 bunch fresh parsley, chopped
2 medium onions, chopped
salt, pepper
$1/4$ teaspoon ground cloves
4 cloves garlic
1 15- or 16-ounce can diced tomatoes, preferably Mexican style

$1/4$ cup diced canned chilis, drained
2 cups water
$1/2$ ounce unsweetened chocolate, finely chopped

Layer meat in a Dutch oven with remaining ingredients except chocolate. Cover and cook 7 to 8 hours buried in well-started coals or in the oven at 250°F. Add the chocolate and stir until melted. Serves 8 to 10.

Serve with fluffy white rice, a marinated vegetable salad, cornbread, and a flan or custard for dessert.

Fruited Lamb

1 pound lean lamb for stew, trimmed of all fat
flour
oil
$1^{1}/2$ cups dried fruit, diced (apples, cranberries, raisins, apricots, prunes)

4 tablespoons lemon juice
$1/4$ cup honey
1 cup orange or apple juice
$1/2$ teaspoon apple pie spice
1 tablespoon cornstarch

Dredge lamb in flour and brown in hot oil in a Dutch oven over high heat. Remove from heat and add remaining ingredients except cornstarch. Cover and cook 8 to 10 hours buried in well-started coals or at 250°F in a conventional or convection oven. Remove from oven. Add enough water to the cornstarch to make a paste and stir into the hot meat mixture over a medium flame. Stir until juices thicken and clear. Serves 4.

Serve with aromatic rice, pita triangles, coarsely shredded apple-cabbage slaw, and iced watermelon for dessert.

Forgotten Stew

Many versions of this forgiving stew have been published over the years, and the recipe is worth repeating here. One of its best features for the RV cook is that it throws together in one pot and cooks, forgotten, until supper time.

1 16-ounce can stewed tomatoes	4 to 5 ribs celery, coarsely sliced
1 cup water (part red wine if you like)	3 medium onions, diced
1 beef bouillon cube	2 tablespoons Dijon mustard
2 teaspoons dried Italian seasoning	1/4 cup quick-cooking tapioca
3 pounds lean, boneless stew beef	1 12-ounce can mushrooms, drained
1 pound carrots, peeled and cut into chunks	1 10-ounce package frozen peas, thawed
	salt, pepper

campfire cooking

Mix everything but mushrooms, peas, salt, and pepper in a large Dutch oven or covered casserole. Bury in well-started coals for the day or bake at 250°F for 8 to 9 hours (to shorten cooking time, bake at 325°F for 3 to 4 hours). Stir in mushrooms and peas, salt and pepper to taste, and heat through. Serves 10.

Serve with cloverleaf rolls or hot garlic bread, with crunchy red apples for dessert.

Creamy Chicken

Of all the shortcut recipes that call for condensed cream soup, this one keeps its secret best. There is something about the combination of the sherry, soup, and sour cream that makes the flavor hard to pin down, so nobody will guess you're a cook who takes shortcuts.

8 boneless chicken breast halves
1 can condensed cream of chicken soup
1 soup-can sherry
1 soup-can sour cream

Roll chicken into bundles and arrange in one layer in a Dutch oven or casserole. Whisk together other ingredients, pour over chicken, and bake, tightly covered, at 325°F for 3 hours or 4 to 5 hours buried in hot coals. Serve over rice. Serves 8.

Variation: Pound chicken breasts flat and wrap around several leaves of dried chipped beef. Proceed as above.

Complete the menu with fresh fruit cup, hot rolls, steamed carrots, and a dessert of canned vanilla pudding topped with finely chopped peanut butter cups.

Milepost Minestrone

1 20-ounce package frozen
  mixed vegetables
3 to 4 fully cooked breakfast
  links, thinly sliced
1 16-ounce can tomato sauce
2 cups water
1 can beef broth
1 15- or 16-ounce can diced
  tomatoes
1 medium onion, diced
2 15- or 16-ounce cans red
  kidney beans
2 tablespoons Italian seasoning
  (basil, oregano)
1 cup uncooked macaroni or
  other pasta

campfire cooking

Put everything in a Dutch oven or ovenproof casserole, stir once, cover, and bake at 275°F for 3 to 4 hours or bury for half a day in hot coals. Add salt and pepper to taste. Ladle into soup plates. Serves 4 to 5.

Serve with crusty bread with saucers of olive oil for dipping, a tossed salad, and ice-cream bars for a walking dessert.

All-Day Meatball Sandwiches

2 32-ounce jars spaghetti sauce
3 pounds very lean ground
   beef or turkey
1 medium onion, diced
1/3 cup grated Parmesan
   cheese
2 tablespoons Italian seasoning
   (basil, oregano)

1 teaspoon salt
dash pepper
1 single-serving packet plain
   instant oatmeal
12 hoagie or sub buns

Pour spaghetti sauce into an ovenproof casserole or a Dutch oven. Wearing disposable gloves, combine meat, onion, cheese, seasonings, and oatmeal and form into golf ball–size meatballs (about 36). Drop carefully into the sauce, cover, and bury in coals for the day or bake at 250°F for 6 to 8 hours. Split buns. Using a slotted spoon, carefully fish meatballs out of sauce and put 3 in each bun. Top with a little sauce. Makes 12 sandwiches.

Complete the meal with broccoli slaw, potato chips, and a dessert of piña colada bread pudding (see next page).

Refrigerate any leftover sauce. Tomorrow, make pizzas for lunch: spread the sauce on English muffin halves, top with grated cheese, and bake at 425°F until heated through.

The Slowest Fajitas in the West

1 1/2 pounds London broil
1 large onion, diced
1 green pepper, seeded and
    cut into strips
1 red pepper, seeded and cut
    into strips
1 8-ounce can diced tomatoes
2 tablespoons minced garlic

1 tablespoon chili powder
1 teaspoon cumin
1 teaspoon coriander
dash salt
12 large flour tortillas
sour cream, guacamole, grated
    cheese, salsa
chopped cilantro (optional)

Cut London broil into about 6 chunks and place in an ovenproof casserole or Dutch oven. Add vegetables and seasonings and stir once. Cover and bake 4 to 5 hours at 275°F or bury in hot coals for the day. Remove meat, place on a disposable cutting sheet, and pull apart with two forks. Divide among the tortillas and add the accompaniments. Serves 6.

Piña Colada Bread Pudding

This is a rich, show-off dessert for the family that dotes on Dutch oven cookery. It's a delicious dessert, but leftover pudding also makes a yummy breakfast. Eat it cold or heat in the microwave.

1 loaf sandwich bread (square
    slices)
1/2 teaspoon nutmeg
2 sticks butter, at room
    temperature
2 cups sugar

8 eggs
2 15- or 16-ounce cans
    crushed pineapple, drained
    (reserve juice)
2 teaspoons rum flavoring
about 1 cup flaked coconut

Remove crusts from bread (scatter them for the birds) and cut bread into cubes. Put in a buttered Dutch oven and sprinkle with nutmeg. Using a bowl and wooden spoon or an electric mixer, beat together butter and sugar, gradually adding eggs, rum flavoring, and pineapple juice. Gently fold egg mixture, coconut, and crushed pineapple into bread cubes. Cover and bake 4 hours at 275°F, 1 hour at 350°F, or bury in hot coals for the afternoon. Serve plain or with regular or fat-free cream. Serves 6 to 8.

campfire cooking

Thirteen

Celebrate Vegetables

F resh vegetables are one of travel's greatest joys. Stop at roadside stands to buy the biggest, best, and freshest of the harvest. Try chayote, yucca, weirdly shaped squash, new tomato hybrids, Jerusalem artichokes, horseradish you have to grate yourself, and sweet corn more savory than can be found in any supermarket. If you don't recognize it, try it anyway, and make a new friend as the farmer tells you how to prepare it.

One of the best corn dishes we ever had was in the backwoods of North Carolina, where a farm wife gave us a sheaf of field corn, and promised it would be good if I prepared it as she suggested. (It was heavenly.)

In the South, come to terms with the various greens harvested there. In the North, discover fiddleheads. In the Southwest, learn the many uses of prickly pear cactus, tomatillos, and blue cornmeal. Food discoveries are among travel's greatest pleasures. Vegetables, low in cost and calories, lead them all.

Halve acorn squash and place cut side down on a greased cookie sheet. Bake at 350°F until tender. Turn over, fill hollows with apple pie filling from a can, and return to oven to heat through. Serve as a side dish with pork chops.

Vegetables as a Side Dish

Mystery Appetizer

Although it tastes like a feast of creamy spices, this velvety dip is made with inexpensive, low-cal eggplant. Even a heaping helping of 4 or 5 table-spoons is only about 50 calories. This is best made ahead of time to let flavors blend.

1 pound eggplant
2 cloves garlic
several scallions
2 teaspoons vinegar
2 teaspoons soy sauce
1 teaspoon olive oil
$1/4$ cup chopped parsley

Cut eggplant in half lengthwise, make a slit in each half, and slip in a peeled garlic clove. Place cut sides down on paper towels in the microwave. Bake on High 12 to 16 minutes or until soft. Let cool, then scoop out flesh and put in a food processor with the remaining ingredients. Chill, but let come to room temperature before serving. Stir and sprinkle with chopped parsley at the last minute. Makes $1^1/2$ cups.

Serve with crackers or raw vegetables for dipping.

Stir-Fry Asparagus

$1^1/2$ pounds fresh asparagus, cut into 1-inch-long pieces
2 cloves garlic, mashed
3 tablespoons peanut oil*
1 hard-boiled egg
salt, pepper

vegetables

Stir-fry garlic in oil over medium heat until softened. Careful! It burns easily. Turn heat to high and stir-fry asparagus until crisp-tender. Sprinkle with finely chopped egg and add salt and pepper to taste. Serves 6.

*Because of its higher flash point, peanut oil is preferred for stir-fry dishes. Note, however, that some people have life-threatening peanut allergies.

Cabbage Casserole

With this in the oven and meat on the grill, you have a complete menu. Just add salad, hot bread, and a fruited gelatin dessert.

2 pounds cabbage, coarsely shredded	1 teaspoon salt
1 28-ounce can diced tomatoes	$1/2$ cup seasoned breadcrumbs
1 small onion, chopped	2 ounces grated cheddar cheese
1 clove garlic, minced	2 tablespoons butter, melted
1 cup uncooked rice, cooked to make 3 cups	

Put cabbage and tomatoes in a saucepan. Add onion and garlic and bring to a boil. Cover and simmer 5 minutes. Add rice and salt and place in a buttered casserole. Sprinkle with breadcrumbs and cheese and drizzle with melted butter. Bake 45 minutes at 375°F. Serves 8.

Crusty Potato Casserole

1 large sweet onion, diced
1 16-ounce bag frozen hash browns
4 ounces grated jack cheese
pinch salt
dash pepper
1 egg, beaten
$1/2$ cup milk
2 tablespoons butter

vegetables

Combine everything in a greased casserole, ending with the butter (in bits), and bake at 350°F for 20 to 30 minutes or until the top is lightly browned. Let stand 5 minutes before serving. Serves 4.

Creamy Potato Casserole

Long, slow cooking allows the potatoes to steep and flavors to blend.

6 servings instant mashed potatoes
12 ounces creamy cottage cheese
$1/3$ cup sour cream
1 tablespoon dried onion flakes
1 tablespoon dried chives
melted butter

Using a heavy saucepan with a tight, heavy lid, prepare mashed potatoes according to package directions. Fold in cottage cheese, sour cream, onion flakes, and chives and drizzle with melted butter. Cover and heat in the same pan, over a very low flame, until hot through. Serves 6 to 8.

For a more crusty result, bake uncovered in a buttered casserole at 350°F for 30 minutes.

Milemaker Cream Sauce, Master Recipe

Use your imagination with this sauce, varying it each time to find all the best combinations for your family's tastes.

1 can condensed soup
$1/2$ cup milk
$1/4$ to $1/2$ teaspoon seasoning

Try cream of tomato with basil, cream of mushroom with curry powder, cream of celery with dill weed, cream of chicken with thyme, and broccoli cheese with lemon pepper. Whisk together soup and milk while heating gently in a saucepan over low flame or in the microwave, add seasoning to taste, and spoon over hot cooked vegetables. Makes about 2 cups.

vegetables

Oven-fry slabs of eggplant, green tomato, zucchini, or yellow squash after dipping in beaten egg, then seasoned cornmeal. Place on well-oiled baking sheet and bake at 450°F, turning once, 30 minutes or until tender.

Vegetable One-Dish Can-Can

Canning doesn't improve vegetables and, in many instances, makes them almost inedible. Still, canned foods are useful as backup staples, and their taste can be improved. Canned potatoes taste better if drained, rinsed, and drained again. To develop the taste even further, fry in bacon fat or real butter.

Most canned vegetables taste better if served cold with a vinaigrette dressing or combined with other fresh or canned vegetables. This recipe can be thrown together in an emergency with foods kept on your shelf, and it makes a complete accompaniment for any plain meat. It's best with freshly grated Romano or Parmesan.

1 large onion, diced
1 green pepper, diced
2 ribs celery, diced
1 tablespoon olive oil
1 16-ounce can sliced potatoes, drained and rinsed
1 16-ounce can stewed tomatoes
1 16-ounce can spinach, drained
1/4 cup grated Romano or Parmesan cheese

Sauté onion, pepper, and celery in olive oil in a big skillet, then add potatoes and sauté several minutes more. Add tomatoes with their juice and bring to a boil to reduce liquid slightly, then gently stir in spinach to heat through. Sprinkle with cheese and serve. Serves 6.

vegetables

Hot and Creamy Potato Salad

2 pounds new potatoes, scrubbed and cut into chunks
$2/3$ cup mayonnaise
1 small sweet onion, minced
1 pint cherry tomatoes, quartered
1 8-ounce can whole baby carrots, julienned
$1/3$ cup real bacon bits

Boil potatoes until fork tender. Drain and toss with remaining ingredients. Serve warm. Serves 6 to 8.

Carrot Custard

1 pound carrots, sliced	dash pepper
1 small onion, diced	dash nutmeg
1 cup milk	2 tablespoons butter, melted
2 eggs	8 individual saltine crackers,
1 teaspoon salt	crushed

Cook carrots and onion together until tender, drain well, and mash. Beat in milk, eggs, seasonings, cracker crumbs, and melted butter. If you're making this at home for baking on the go, transfer to a buttered casserole and refrigerate up to 2 days. To proceed, stir and bake at 350°F for about 35 minutes or until set. Serves 4 to 6.

Creamy Beets

1 15- or 16-ounce can quartered beets
2 tablespoons sour cream
$1/4$ cup zesty Italian salad dressing

Heat the beets thoroughly, drain well, and toss with the remaining ingredients. Serves 2 to 3.

vegetables

Turn cornbread mix into a zesty vegetable side dish. Sauté 2 large onions in butter until soft. Spread in 9-inch square pan and cover with cornbread batter. Bake according to package directions, until bread tests done, and serve with a spoon.

Bootstrap Potatoes

These baked potatoes are crusty and showy and dress up a meal of burgers, meatloaf, or chops. Peel and boil the potatoes when you have time, several days in advance if you like. Tuck them away in the refrigerator for this treat.

6 large Idaho baking potatoes
soft butter
1 cup cornflake crumbs
12 strips bacon

Peel potatoes and boil them whole until just barely tender. Don't overcook. Chill. Using soft butter or margarine and your bare hands, coat potatoes and roll them in cornflake crumbs. Wrap each with 2 slices of bacon in a cross, tucking ends in well, and bake on a cookie sheet at 375°F about 20 minutes or until the bacon is just crisp. Serves 6.

Vegetables as a Main Dish

Spinach-Stuffed Shells

This is the ideal first-night-out dinner because you can assemble it completely at home. Whisk it out of the refrigerator and into the oven. By the time you're hooked up and settled in, it will be hot, fragrant, and ready to eat.

vegetables

2 10-ounce packages frozen chopped spinach, thawed and drained
8 ounces grated mozzarella
16 ounces cottage cheese
$^1/_2$ cup grated Parmesan cheese
3 tablespoons dried onion flakes
1 tablespoon dried parsley flakes
1 teaspoon mixed Italian herbs
1 32-ounce jar spaghetti sauce
additional grated Parmesan
12 jumbo uncooked pasta shells

Squeeze any excess moisture from spinach. Mix with all other ingredients except sauce, additional cheese, and shells. Boil shells until barely soft. Cool and stuff with spinach mixture. Pour half the spaghetti sauce into a 13-by-9-by-2-inch baking dish and arrange shells on top. Cover with remaining sauce and sprinkle with cheese. Cover with plastic wrap and refrigerate. Bake, uncovered, at 350°F for 45 to 60 minutes. Serves 4 to 6.

Baked Potato Campfire Dinner

4 large baking potatoes
1 9-ounce package frozen creamed spinach, thawed
pinch nutmeg
4 eggs
grated Parmesan cheese (optional)

Scrub potatoes, wrap in foil, and bake on the grill until tender. Remove from grill and carefully open the foil, leaving each potato surrounded by a "boat" of foil. Cut a cross in the top of each potato and spread open. Spoon spinach into potatoes, make a nest in each bed of spinach, sprinkle very lightly with nutmeg, and break an egg into each. Put potatoes back on the grill or in the coals, covering lightly with the foil if it's windy. Bake just until eggs are poached to the desired doneness. Sprinkle with cheese and eat right out of the foil. Serves 4.

Complete this meal with raw vegetable sticks, a low-calorie yogurt dip, and big oatmeal raisin cookies for dessert. No dishes to wash!

vegetables

Squash Flapjacks

2 cups shredded zucchini or summer squash
$^1/_2$ cup flour
2 eggs, slightly beaten
salt, pepper
oil

Mix everything except oil in a bowl. Cook like pancakes in a hot skillet with about $^1/_4$ inch oil. Brown on both sides, drain on paper towels, and serve at once. Serves 2 to 4.

Serve these with ketchup for a simple supper. Add sausage patties if you want some meat, steamed carrots for color contrast, and hot apple pie for dessert.

Cheese-Topped Baked Potatoes

4 to 6 large baking potatoes	1 small onion, minced
4 tablespoons real bacon bits (optional)	3 tablespoons instant-blend flour
	1 teaspoon Dijon mustard
Cheese Sauce	1 12-ounce can or bottle beer
$^1/_2$ stick butter	12 ounces grated cheddar
1 teaspoon minced garlic	cheese

Bake potatoes, cut a cross in the centers, and squeeze to open and fluff them. To make sauce, sauté garlic and onion in butter, then blend in flour, mustard, and beer. Stir over low heat until thickened. Gradually add cheese, cooking just until it melts. Sauce potatoes with cheese mixture and sprinkle each with a tablespoon of bacon bits. Serves 4 to 6.

vegetables

Cut up and fry 3 slices bacon. Pour off all but 3 tablespoons fat, and stir-fry a medium red cabbage, coarsely grated. Season to taste with vinegar, salt, pepper, and a touch of sugar. Stir the bacon bits into the slaw and serve warm or at room temperature.

Ratatouille Pizza

1 tube refrigerated pizza
    dough (12-inch crust)
1/4 cup olive oil
1 small eggplant, peeled and
    diced
1 medium zucchini, diced
1 medium onion, diced
2 teaspoons minced garlic

2 teaspoons mixed Italian
    herbs
1 8-ounce can tomato sauce
pinch salt
freshly grated Parmesan
    cheese
4 ounces grated mozzarella
    cheese

Unroll pizza dough onto a lightly greased pizza pan. In a roomy skillet, sauté vegetables in olive oil until they are just tender. Stir in seasonings and tomato sauce and spread over dough. Sprinkle with Parmesan and mozzarella. Bake at 450°F for 20 minutes, or until cheese is melted and dough is brown around the edges. Serves 4 to 6.

Baked Onions

When apple-sweet onions are available along roadsides in Georgia, Florida, and Texas, buy them in 10-pound sacks because you'll use them cooked and raw in so many ways.

4 jumbo sweet onions
2 teaspoons melted butter

Toppings
1 can any condensed cream
    soup mixed with 1 teaspoon
    curry powder

1/3 cup firmly packed brown
    sugar with a dash of
    cayenne pepper
1 cup sour cream with 1 teaspoon dill weed
1/2 cup barbecue sauce (plus
    1/4 cup more after foil is
    removed)

Peel and trim onions, cut in half, and arrange cut side up in a buttered casserole. Drizzle with butter, then spread with only one of the toppings. Cover with foil and bake at 350°F for 20 to 30 minutes or until onions are just tender but still hold their shape. Remove foil and bake another 5 minutes. Serves 8.

vegetables

Tomato and Celery Scallop

2 slices bacon, cut up
1 large onion, diced
1 bunch celery, cleaned and sliced
1 16-ounce can stewed tomatoes, chopped
1 tablespoon instant-blend flour
2 tablespoons water

In a roomy skillet, fry bacon until done, then add onion and celery and cook until they begin to get tender. Add tomatoes, cover, and simmer over low heat until vegetables are soft. Mix flour and water together to blend, then add to vegetables. Bring to a boil and cook until sauce has thickened. Serves 4 to 6.

Eggplant Surprise

2 pounds eggplant, peeled and diced
2 onions, diced
2 tablespoons butter
1 cup applesauce
salt, pepper

Cook eggplant and onions in a covered saucepan, with a little water, until very tender. Drain and mash with butter and applesauce. Add salt and pepper to taste.

Gussied-Up Canned Carrots

When you're out of fresh carrots, delve into your cupboards for canned. Then make them sit up and sing by fixing them this way. Onions, fried in real butter, are another good way to refresh canned carrots, potatoes, spinach, or green beans.

vegetables

2 to 3 ribs celery, cut into chunks
1 tablespoon butter
1 tablespoon sesame seeds
1 15- or 16-ounce can whole baby carrots, drained

Sauté celery in butter over low heat until crisp-tender. Add sesame seeds and continue sautéing, then add carrots and stir-fry over low heat until well heated. Serves 4 to 6.

Creamed Potatoes

2 pounds potatoes, peeled and diced
2 tablespoons butter
2 cups milk
5 tablespoons instant-blend flour
freshly ground pepper
$1/2$ teaspoon dill weed or 2 tablespoons freshly grated Parmesan cheese

Cook potatoes in salted water until just tender but still hold their shape. Drain, then stir in butter. Mix milk and flour together, pour over potatoes, and cook over low flame, stirring gently, until a thick sauce forms. Add pepper and dill weed or cheese. Serves 8.

Unbeatable Beets

1 pound red cabbage, coarsely shredded
1 16-ounce can julienned beets, drained
1 16-ounce can pie-sliced apples*
1 teaspoon sugar
salt to taste
2 tablespoons butter

Add a little water to the cabbage and cook cabbage in a covered pot just until tender. Then fold in beets, apples, sugar, and salt. Cook over very low flame until everything is heated through. Top with butter. Serves 6 to 8.

vegetables

*Make sure you buy canned apples, not apple pie filling, which contains sugar and thickener.

Variation: Omit the sugar and add ¼ cup red currant jelly.

The Best Baked Beans

The more varieties of beans I add, the better my guests like my "from scratch" baked beans. And the bigger the crowd, the more different cans of beans I can add. It's my campground potluck favorite, limited only by the size of whatever pot I have available for oven or campfire use.

3 to 4 15- or 16-ounce cans beans (use a variety: canned pork and beans, light and dark red kidney beans, navy beans, pinto beans, black beans, limas, perhaps even some garbanzos and pigeon peas, all in their own juices)

1 16-ounce can pineapple tidbits, with juice
blackstrap molasses
several strips bacon

Mix beans and pineapple bits in a Dutch oven or similar large, oven-proof pot or casserole. Stir in molasses until mixture is a rich, deep brown. Paste a couple of strips of bacon across the top and bake uncovered at 350°F until bacon is done and beans have formed a thick sauce, about 30 to 60 minutes. The longer the baking time, the better, but check occasionally to keep beans from burning or getting too dry. Serves 8 to 10.

Garlic Custard Cups

6 green peppers
3 cloves garlic, minced
2 cups milk
½ teaspoon salt
3 eggs
freshly ground pepper
dash nutmeg

vegetables

Cut tops off peppers and remove seeds. Place peppers in a lightly greased baking pan. If necessary, take a tiny slice off the bottoms so they'll stand upright, but make sure they remain leakproof. Scald milk with minced garlic until a skin forms on top. Beat eggs with salt, pepper, and nutmeg. Strain hot milk into the eggs, beating well, and pour into pepper cups. Bake at 350°F for 20 to 30 minutes or until custard is just set. Serve at once; add meat hot from the grill, if you like. Serves 6.

Bubble and Squeak

A mainstay of British pub fare, this all-in-one vegetable dish is ideal for the space-short RV galley.

1 small onion, diced
3 tablespoons oil (traditionally, beef or bacon fat is used)
2 16-ounce cans sliced potatoes, drained and rinsed
1 16-ounce can sliced carrots, drained
1 small cabbage, shredded
Worcestershire sauce to taste
salt to taste

If you want to use fresh potatoes and carrots instead of canned, cut them up and boil until tender. To proceed, sauté the onion in hot oil or fat in a large skillet. Add the other vegetables and stir-fry until cabbage is wilted and potatoes are lightly browned. Add Worcestershire sauce, then salt if needed. Serves 6 to 8.

Fast Lane

◆ Roll leftover steamed vegetables in crescent roll dough, bake until the rolls are brown and crusty, and serve as a main dish or side dish. Add a cheese sauce if you like.

◆ Steam carrot chunks until tender and toss with a little brown sugar, a few tablespoons of raisins, and a nugget of butter to coat the carrots.

vegetables

◆ Make vegetarian stuffed peppers by filling green pepper halves with canned Spanish rice. Sprinkle with grated cheese and bake until the peppers are crisp-tender.

◆ Make a zesty vegetarian pizza by spreading toasted English muffin halves with pesto (from the grocer's refrigerated section), then top with bits of cooked vegetables. Bake at 425°F just until heated.

◆ Fill a big buttered casserole with drained canned sweet potatoes and spread with canned apple pie filling. Bake until heated through.

◆ Make a two-in-one vegetable by boiling potatoes with turnips, cabbage, or carrots. Mash with plenty of butter and season to taste.

◆ Make white sauce from a package and fold in quartered whole potatoes from a can and 2 cups frozen peas, thawed. Heat through.

vegetables

Fourteen

Your Salad Days

The crunch of lettuce, bursting with moistness. The tang of freshly picked nasturtium leaves. Tender dandelion shoots, young mustard greens, and pokeweed salad made under the direction of a native who knows its secrets. . . .

Salads made fresh from local produce are another way to translate travel into mealtime pleasure. Dare to discover new greens and ingredients as you go. Locals love to talk about their regional specialties, enriching your roster of friends as your knowledge grows.

This chapter is divided into two parts. One lists main-dish salads and the other suggests salads to accompany the meal. Many of them are well suited for make-and-take preparation. Arrange the salad in a lidded plastic container with whatever garnishes you like and refrigerate. At mealtime, simply pop off the lid and put the presentation on the table or serve in individual lettuce cups.

> Wash all salad greens well at home, drain well, wrap in clean linen dishtowels, and place in plastic bags with plenty of air (as a protective cushion). Kept in the refrigerator, they'll stay crisp for days.

Salads to Make the Meal

Beefsteak Salad

2 pounds sirloin steak, seasoned and broiled to taste
1 pound fresh mushrooms, sliced
2 big, ripe tomatoes, seeded and diced
1 sweet onion, in rings
1 small green pepper, cut into wedges
1 small red pepper, cut into wedges
1 14-ounce can hearts of palm, chopped
$1/2$ cup Italian dressing
lettuce cups or shredded lettuce

Cool the steak, chill, and slice very thin across the grain. Combine meat and vegetables in a large bowl. Toss with dressing and refrigerate. To serve, toss again and spoon into lettuce cups or onto a bed of shredded lettuce. Serves 6 to 8.

Paella Salad

1 5-ounce package yellow rice mix
8 ounces cooked, cleaned shrimp
1 6- to 8-ounce can crabmeat, drained and picked over
1 $6^{1}/_{2}$-ounce can white-meat chicken
1 medium tomato, diced

$1/2$ cup fresh or frozen green peas, thawed
3 to 4 scallions, thinly sliced
lettuce

Dressing
$1/4$ cup vinegar
$1/4$ cup olive oil
$1/2$ teaspoon curry powder

Cook rice according to package directions (omit butter). Cool. Combine dressing ingredients and shake well. Lightly toss seafood, chicken, and vegetables with the dressing and serve atop a bed of lettuce. Garnish with lemon wedges. Serves 4.

Complete a cold meal by serving slabs of a hearty whole-grain bread with sweet butter and fresh fruit for dessert. In cooler weather, start the meal with a cream soup and end it with mugs of hot Jack Daniels coffee: mix half a shot glass Jack Daniels with half a shot glass Amaretto, pour into mug, fill with hot coffee, and top with whipped cream.

Couscous Salad

You can substitute rice, but it's fun to experiment with couscous, a small, pastalike wheat product used in North African cooking. Almost all supermarkets stock this now and it keeps on the shelf as well as any pasta. This exotic, tangy salad is served warm or at room temperature.

12 ounces boneless, skinless
   chicken breast
water
1 carrot, finely chopped
1 cup uncooked couscous
6 radishes, diced
1/2 cup raisins
3 to 4 scallions, finely sliced
1 tablespoon peanuts, chopped

Dressing
2 tablespoons poaching liquid
2 tablespoons lemon juice
1 tablespoon olive oil
1 teaspoon cumin
1 teaspoon turmeric
salt, pepper to taste

Poach chicken in about 2 cups boiling water until cooked through. Drain, reserving 2 tablespoons of the liquid for the dressing, and set remaining liquid aside. Cool chicken and cut into bite-size morsels. Bring 1 1/2 cups of the poaching liquid to a boil, stir in the carrot and couscous, cover, and remove from heat. Let stand 5 minutes, then fluff with a fork. Toss together couscous mixture, chicken, and remaining ingredients. Whisk together dressing ingredients and toss with couscous mixture. Serves 4 to 6.

salads

Add a few tablespoons of salad dressing to a plastic bag of salad greens, toss, and serve. Throw away the bag. No salad bowl to wash!

Pasta Crab Salad

This is easily made at home. Pile it into a pretty carry-and-serve container and keep it cold. Serve within a day or two.

16 ounces seashell pasta, cooked and drained
12 to 16 ounces imitation crabmeat, cut up
2 hard-boiled eggs, diced
3 ribs celery, diced
1 large carrot, grated
$^1/_2$ green pepper, diced
$^1/_2$ red pepper, diced
1 small sweet onion, diced
$^1/_2$ cup frozen green peas, thawed
$^1/_2$ cup yogurt
$^1/_2$ cup mayonnaise

Mix pasta, crabmeat, eggs, and vegetables in a large bowl. Whisk together yogurt and mayonnaise and toss with crabmeat mixture. Add salt and pepper to taste. Garnish with lemon wedges. Serves 6 to 8.

Complete each plate with a slice of chilled tomato aspic, a slab of French bread, and a pat of sweet butter. Add a dry white wine if you like. Fresh cantaloupe goes well for dessert.

Macaroni Salad, Master Recipe

Macaroni is a mainstay, especially during the summer when you can make a mountain of macaroni salad at home and bring a batch out of the refrigerator for lunch daily during the first two or three days of your trip. Make sure the refrigerator stays at 38 to 40°F, and package the salad in batches so you take out only what you need for each meal, keeping the rest cold.

The first day, serve it with deli cold cuts and garnish with spiced apple rings. The second, strew it with drained tuna and serve with sliced cranberry sauce. The third, mix in some diced canned ham and serve with pineapple rings.

salads

16 ounces uncooked macaroni
1 cup mayonnaise
1 cup yogurt
1 teaspoon dried dill weed
1 sweet red onion, diced
1 green pepper, diced
1 red pepper, diced
3 tablespoons sweet pickle relish
3 ribs celery, diced

Cook macaroni until just tender and drain. While it's cooking, mix other ingredients in a big bowl. Fold in macaroni, divide into storage containers, and chill at once. Makes 3 batches (4 servings each).

Tofu-Egg Salad

This makes enough for a crowd, and nobody will guess that low-fat bean curd has been used as a partial egg stand-in.

1 8-ounce block firm tofu
6 to 8 hard-boiled eggs
6 ribs celery, diced
1 small onion, minced
2 to 3 tablespoons pickle relish (optional)
1 small carrot, finely chopped
1 cup nonfat yogurt
mayonnaise

Mash tofu and eggs together and fold in celery, onion, relish, and carrot. Add yogurt and stir well, then add mayonnaise to achieve desired moistness. Serves 6 to 8.

Serve by the scoop as a main-dish salad or use it as a sandwich filling.

salads

Golden Glow Salad

2 cups uncooked carrot rotelle or other carrot pasta
6 hard-boiled eggs
1 large yellow pepper, diced
1 medium Spanish onion, minced
4 ounces grated cheddar cheese
1 tablespoon Dijon mustard
1 8-ounce carton nonfat lemon yogurt
mayonnaise

Boil pasta in salted water until just tender. Drain. Fold in remaining ingredients, adding mayo little by little until moist enough to suit family tastes. Serve on lettuce-lined plates if you like. Serves 6 to 8.

Use-Your-Noodle Salad

1 16-ounce package shredded cabbage for slaw (or shred your own)
1 medium green pepper, diced
3 to 4 scallions, finely sliced
8 ounces deli ham or breast of turkey, sliced into matchsticks
1 4- to 6-ounce can or package chow mein noodles
1/2 cup Italian dressing

Pile vegetables into a roomy bowl. Add the meat with half the chow mein noodles. Toss with the dressing, sprinkle with remaining noodles, and serve at once. Serves 4 to 6.

When you finish a big jar of pickles, bring the leftover juice to a boil and pour it over a container of carrot sticks. Refrigerate overnight, and you will have have dilly carrots.

salads

Sausage Salad

16 ounces shredded green cabbage
16 ounces shredded red cabbage
2 medium cucumbers, seeded and sliced
2 pounds mixed deli meats, cubed*
2 tomatoes, seeded and diced
1 16-ounce can sliced potatoes, rinsed and drained
1 small sweet onion, minced
$^1/_2$ cup Italian dressing

At home, place cabbages and cucumber in a colander. Sprinkle with salt and let stand 30 minutes. Drain, pressing lightly to remove excess moisture. Toss cabbages, cucumber, meat, and remaining vegetables lightly with dressing and refrigerate. Toss again just before serving. Serves 8 to 10.

*Get a good variety of fully cooked deli meats, including smoked sausage, wursts, salami, kielbasa, turkey breast, boiled ham, etc. Have them sliced $^1/_2$ inch thick.

Complete the meal with buttered pumpernickel rolls, perhaps a mug of instant soup if the weather is cold, and individually wrapped pie-style cookies.

Salads to Go with the Meal

Right Now Corn Relish

Corn relish is a perfect complement to almost any main dish and is a lifesaver when you're boondocking and run out of fresh salad makings. Stir up this tangy, instant version of an old favorite. It goes well with any grilled meat.

1 15- or 16-ounce can whole-kernel corn with red peppers, drained
1 rib celery
1 small red onion, minced
$^1/_4$ green pepper, minced
1 tablespoon brown sugar
$^1/_3$ cup vinegar
1 tablespoon prepared mustard
salt to taste

Combine all ingredients in a serving dish. You can serve at once, but the relish will improve if chilled. Makes $2^1/_2$ cups.

Pasta Salad, Master Recipe

Cook 8 ounces of your favorite pasta, then add your choice of one or more of the following:

4 ounces fresh snow peas, trimmed
1 medium sweet onion (Vidalia, Texas Sweet), diced
2 ribs celery, diced
1 red and 1 green pepper, diced
2 large carrots, grated
$^1/_2$ cup frozen peas, thawed
2 to 3 canned artichoke hearts, drained and quartered
2 medium tomatoes, seeded and diced
$^1/_4$ cup canned sliced ripe or stuffed olives, drained
$^1/_3$ cup pecans or cashews

Master Dressing
$^1/_2$ cup oil
$^1/_4$ cup vinegar
salt, pepper to taste
fresh or dried herbs to taste
other seasonings to taste
(1 tablespoon Dijon mustard, 1 tablespoon soy sauce, pinch ginger, dash onion or garlic salt, 1 teaspoon sugar, 1 tablespoon tomato paste)

Whisk ingredients together in a large bowl, add salad ingredients, and toss lightly. Serves at least 6 (depending on your additions).

My first choice for oil is always virgin olive oil, but there are countless other choices such as walnut oil or oils infused with herbs. Experiment too with different vinegars or lemon or lime juice.

Marinated Fennel Salad

Fennel tastes somewhat like celery with a faint taste of anise. This salad is something different, refreshingly crisp and cold.

2 large fennel bulbs	*Dressing*
1 cucumber	2 tablespoons vinegar
8 ounces radishes, sliced	2 teaspoons lemon juice
2 scallions, sliced	6 tablespoons oil
salt	

Wash, trim, and halve fennel bulbs and slice very thin. Peel, seed, and slice cucumber and sprinkle with salt. Let stand 45 minutes, then drain on paper towels. Toss all the vegetables together. Shake vinegar, lemon juice, and oil together and pour over vegetables. Toss again and refrigerate. Garnish with chopped fresh parsley if you have some. Serves 4 to 6.

Slow-Lane Slaw

There are many variations of this coleslaw, which keeps in the refrigerator for a week or more. This version has no oil. Its secret is a cooked dressing that does not get watery. I make a large batch of it at home using the food processor, and vary it during the week by topping it with diced apple one day, and grated carrots with a sprinkling of fresh chopped parsley the next.

1 large cabbage, about 3	*Dressing*
pounds, shredded	1 cup sugar
1 medium sweet onion, diced	1 cup vinegar
3 ribs celery, diced	1 teaspoon turmeric
1 green pepper, diced	1 teaspoon mustard seed

salads

Cut the vegetables fine or coarse, as you like them, and combine in a large bowl. Combine dressing ingredients in a small saucepan and bring to a boil. While still warm, toss with vegetables. Refrigerate for 24 hours to allow flavors to blend. Mix before serving. Serves 12.

Sticks and Stones Salad

This salad also improves as it marinates. It's made from canned vegetables, so it's the perfect fallback when you're out of lettuce.

1 16-ounce can whole green
   beans, drained
1 2-ounce jar pimientos, drained
4 ribs celery, julienned
. 1 15- or 16-ounce can baby
   carrots or baby corn, drained
1 green pepper, diced
1 large sweet onion, in rings

Dressing
1 cup sugar
^{1}/2 cup salad oil
^{3}/4 cup vinegar
1 teaspoon salt

Combine canned and fresh vegetables. Bring dressing ingredients to a boil and pour over vegetables. Cool and refrigerate several hours or overnight. Mix before serving. Serves 6 to 8.

Bread Salad #2

Crunchy texture contrast is the appeal of this crusty salad, so serve it immediately after mixing. It goes well with cold cuts, wursts, pasta casseroles, or any hot meat. To turn it into a main-dish salad, add cubes of Swiss cheese, Vermont cheddar, or Monterey Jack.

2 cups packaged croutons, plain or seasoned
3 large fresh tomatoes, diced
^{1}/3 cup Italian dressing

Toss croutons with tomatoes and dressing and serve at once. Serves 4 to 6.

salads

Stretch dwindling lettuce supplies by adding well-drained canned foods to tossed salads. Good additions include artichoke hearts, whole green beans, garbanzos, sliced beets, black beans, plain or marinated mushrooms, or baby carrots.

Vegetables Vinaigrette

Make this a day or two ahead of time at home and serve instead of a hot vegetable with meat from the grill. It is tangy and colorful. To make a heartier salad to serve as a vegetarian main dish, use a larger can of garbanzos.

1 head cauliflower, cut into
   bite-size pieces
1 head broccoli, cut into bite-
   size pieces
3 carrots, diced
3 ribs celery, diced
1 green pepper, diced
1 red pepper, diced
1 bunch scallions, diced
1 8-ounce can garbanzos,
   drained
1/4 cup canned sliced ripe
   olives, drained
lettuce

Dressing
1 cup wine vinegar
1 cup water
1/3 cup virgin olive oil
2 to 3 tablespoons minced garlic
1 tablespoon dried parsley
1 1/2 teaspoons mixed Italian
   herbs
freshly ground pepper
pinch salt

Combine dressing ingredients. Place all the vegetables (except garbanzos and olives) in a large pot, pour on dressing, and bring to a boil. Cover and turn off heat. Let cool and turn into a covered container. Refrigerate several hours or overnight. To serve, drain dressing into a small pitcher, stir garbanzos and olives into vegetable mixture, and serve in lettuce cups or on a bed of shredded lettuce. Pass the dressing, which also goes well as a dip for chunks of French bread. Serves 8 to 10.

Fifteen

SOS: Meals from Shelf Staples

There's a snug, smug feeling in knowing that you have an extra meal or two tucked away on board, ready to pull out if you want to linger longer in a pleasant campsite, invite the neighbors in for an impromptu meal, or feed your family if the refrigeration fails. Thanks to modern convenience foods, you can keep a complete menu or two on the shelf.

Plan one complete meal, keep all the ingredients together in the pantry, and don't let yourself raid these supplies for other uses. Here are some complete menus that stay ready without refrigeration, yet come to the galley table looking fresh and coordinated. Of course, if you have fresh foods available, use them to supplement the canned and packaged ones. At the end of your trip, you can use any leftover supplies at home, save them for your next jaunt, or contribute them to a food bank. Extra food on your trips is the most inexpensive insurance you can carry.

Don't forget to include breads among emergency foods. They include hot roll or cornbread mix, packaged crackers and breadsticks, rusks, and canned tortillas or Boston brown bread. Shelf-stable spreads include peanut butter, cheese spreads (unopened), and honey. In the refrigerator, carry tubes of biscuits, breadsticks, and other breads. Watch expiration dates.

Sweet-and-Sour Spam Scramble

2 tablespoons butter
1 16-ounce can whole
   potatoes, rinsed, drained,
   and quartered
1 12-ounce can "light" lunch
   meat, diced

1 16-ounce can garbanzo
   beans, drained
1 16-ounce jar sweet-and-sour
   red cabbage
2 tablespoons dried onion flakes
ranch dressing (optional)

Heat butter to bubbling, then fry potatoes and meat to brown them slightly. Add beans, cabbage, and onion flakes, cover, and steam over low heat until everything is well heated and onion flakes have softened. Spoon onto plates and drizzle lightly with ranch dressing. Serves 4.

Complete the meal with hot bread from a boxed mix, apricot jam, whole asparagus spears heated in the can, and canned tapioca pudding sauced with Tia Maria for dessert.

Salmon Frittata

6 servings instant mashed
   potatoes
2 tablespoons dried onion
   flakes
2 eggs

$\frac{1}{2}$ teaspoon dill weed
2 tablespoons vegetable oil
1 16-ounce can salmon,
   drained and picked over
1 2-ounce jar caviar

Combine onion flakes and potatoes in a bowl and add hot water, milk, and butter as directed on the potato package. Stir with a fork until everything is evenly moistened. Cool. Stir in eggs and dill weed. Heat oil in a big nonstick skillet and spread potato mixture evenly on the bottom. Drop salmon by spoonfuls over potatoes. Press down lightly but do not stir. Cover and cook over low heat until mixture is set and crusty on the bottom. Turn off heat, uncover, and let stand a few minutes for easier serving. Cut into wedges, place on serving plates, and top each with a mound of caviar. Serves 4.

To complete the menu, add pickled beets from a jar, canned peas with small onions, rye hardtack with butter, and canned plum pudding with a jar of hard sauce for dessert.

Black Beans and Rice

2 16-ounce cans black beans
8 ounces canned ham, diced
4 servings hot white rice (instant is OK)
your favorite salsa

Empty beans into a saucepan, juice and all. Add ham and heat until bubbly, seasoning with a touch of salsa. Mix 1 or 2 tablespoons salsa into the hot rice. Spoon rice onto dinner plates, then ladle on the beans. Add more salsa as desired. Serves 4.

Add side dishes of canned tomatoes topped with crunchy croutons, warmed canned tortillas for your bread, and a juicy dessert such as canned mandarin oranges drifted with coconut.

Tortellini A-Go-Go

7 ounces uncooked tricolor tortellini with cheese filling
3 cups water
3 beef bouillon cubes
1 16-ounce can baby carrots, drained
1 16-ounce can zucchini in tomato sauce
1 15 or 16-ounce can cannellini beans, undrained
1 teaspoon mixed Italian herbs

Cook tortellini until just tender. Drain, saving the water to help make up the 3 cups needed, and return to pot. Add the 3 cups water and bring to a boil. Add bouillon cubes, vegetables, and herbs. Simmer until everything is heated through. Add salt and pepper to taste. Serve in shallow soup bowls. Serves 4.

Complete the meal with cheesy breadsticks, a robust red wine, and a salad of canned mushrooms and canned artichoke hearts marinated in a light vinaigrette. For dessert, arrange canned baked apples in serving dishes and drizzle with butterscotch ice-cream topping from a jar.

Chicken-Noodle Mediterranean

If you don't usually carry the following spices on board, measure them out at home, and carry in a zip-top plastic bag or small glass jar.

2 tablespoons dried bell pepper flakes
$1/2$ teaspoon garlic granules
2 tablespoons dried onion flakes
$1/2$ teaspoon mixed Italian herbs

Keep this on your RV's emergency shelf with:

12 ounces egg noodles
2 10-ounce cans chunk chicken
1 28-ounce can stewed tomatoes
1 16-ounce can tiny green peas
$1/4$ cup canned sliced ripe olives, drained

Bring a large pot of water to a boil and cook egg noodles. Drain. Stir in dried herbs and remaining ingredients except peas and olives. Cover and cook over very low heat until everything is heated through. Turn off heat and let stand, covered, 5 minutes more. Gently fold in drained peas and pile into a serving bowl, then strew with olives. Serves 4.

Serve any fresh raw vegetables you can manage, plus buttery crackers, pear halves sprinkled with julienned carrots (canned if necessary), and, for dessert, canned chocolate pudding crowned with raspberry liqueur.

Cranbake Hambake

$1/4$ cup rum or brandy
2 tablespoons raisins
4 servings stovetop stuffing mix
16 ounces canned ham
1 16-ounce can whole cranberry sauce

Heat rum or brandy, add raisins, and leave to soak while you proceed. Prepare stuffing mix according to package directions and pile lightly in a buttered baking pan. Cut ham into 4 slabs and arrange on stuffing. Mash together cranberry sauce and raisin mixture and spread over ham. Bake at 350°F for about 25 minutes, or until everything is well heated and a light crust has begun to form where the stuffing meets the sides of the buttered pan. Serves 4.

Serve with chunky applesauce, succotash from a can, and cornbread made from a mix and drowning in honey butter. For dessert, throw a bag of unsalted popcorn into the microwave. When done, sprinkle lightly with cinnamon sugar.

Cooked Salad Dressing

If you're out of mayonnaise or salad dressing, here's a dressing that doesn't call for the large amounts of oil needed to make real mayo. It's thick, satisfying, and low-fat, too.

$1/3$ cup nonfat powdered milk
1 teaspoon dry mustard
1 teaspoon salt
dash pepper
1 tablespoon flour
1 egg or 2 egg whites
1 cup water
2 tablespoons vinegar
1 tablespoon butter
2 tablespoons sugar or equivalent in sugar substitute

Combine dry ingredients in the top of a double boiler or in a heavy saucepan over very low flame. Beat egg with water and vinegar and add to dry ingredients. Cook, stirring constantly, until smooth and thick. Careful! It burns easily. Remove from heat and add butter and sugar. Makes 2 cups (enough for a big batch of potato salad).

If you keep a can of walnuts and a can of ready-to-eat pitted dates on the shelf, you can make a toothsome dessert by stuffing each date with a walnut half, then rolling it in sugar.

Spaghetti Carbonara

There's always a package of spaghetti in a cupboard somewhere and you can always carry bottled or canned sauce, but here is an unusual sauce that is a change from the same old tomato sauces. Be sure to cook the spaghetti al dente, not too soft.

8 ounces uncooked spaghetti
$1/2$ cup milk
1 teaspoon garlic powder
$1/2$ cup mayo or salad dressing
$1/3$ cup real bacon bits (no substitutes)
$1/3$ cup freshly grated Parmesan or Romano cheese

Whisk together milk, garlic powder, and mayo. Cook spaghetti, drain, and quickly add milk mixture, bacon bits, and cheese. Toss to mix thoroughly. Serve at once. Pass more grated cheese if you like. Serves 4.

Complete the meal with hot bread made from a roll mix, marinated Italian vegetables from a jar (or a green salad if you can manage one), then an SOS shelf dessert like the next recipe.

Honey Rice Dessert

1 cup uncooked brown or white rice
2 cups water
$1/3$ cup raisins
$1/3$ cup chopped walnuts
dash apple pie spice
$1/3$ cup chopped, pitted dates
honey or maple syrup

Add water to rice and cook until soft. Remove from heat and stir in everything but the honey. Cover and set aside so flavors will blend and dates and raisins will absorb moisture. To serve, spoon into bowls and drizzle with honey or syrup. Serves 6 to 8.

Salmon Mousse

Delicate, nutritious salmon in cans stays ready on your shelf until needed. A small jar of mayo, squirreled away for emergencies, is also a good insurance policy because it can be used in so many ways. If you have nonfat yogurt on hand, use a cup of it in this recipe instead. Results will be much the same, but calories will be cut.

1 envelope gelatin
$1/2$ cup boiling water
juice of $1/2$ lemon
1 sweet onion, minced
1 16-ounce can salmon, drained and picked over
1 tablespoon dill weed
dash salt
1 cup mayonnaise
lettuce

Put gelatin in a bowl with lemon juice to soften, then add water and stir until gelatin is dissolved. Mash in salmon and onion, stir in other ingredients, and place in 4-cup pan or bowl. Chill until set, then spoon into lettuce cups. Serves 4.

Serve with lemon wedges, Melba toast, and fresh pineapple fingers.

shelf staples

shelf staples

Beer and Bacon Soup

You don't have to like beer to enjoy this remarkably hearty hot soup. Real bacon bits are one of the mainstays of my emergency shelf.

1 chicken bouillon cube dissolved in 1 cup water
1 12-ounce can or bottle beer
1 16-ounce jar Cheez Whiz
3 tablespoons cornstarch plus water
1 cup water
1 13-ounce can evaporated milk
$1/3$ cup real bacon bits
Tabasco

Heat bouillon mixture in a saucepan and add beer. Meanwhile, in a paper cup, gradually add enough water to the cornstarch to make a thin paste. Add this to beer mixture with the other cup of water. Cook, stirring, until thick. Stir in Cheez Whiz over low heat until mixture is smooth. Stir in evaporated milk and heat. Do not boil. Spoon into bowls and sprinkle generously with bacon bits. Pass Tabasco, which can be added to taste. Serves 4.

Complete the meal with pilot crackers, three-bean salad from a can, and a shelf dessert such as canned fruit topped with instant vanilla pudding.

Can-Can Quiche

This tastes so fresh and fragrant, you'll forget it began with a can of this and a can of that.

1 stick butter
1 cup flour, plus
$2/3$ cup evaporated milk
4 eggs
1 10-ounce can cut asparagus, drained

1 8-ounce can diced carrots and peas, drained
6 ounces chunk ham
1 small onion, minced
$1/2$ cup grated cheddar cheese

Melt butter in a deep 9- or 10-inch pie plate and stir in flour. Use more as needed to make a dough dry enough to press around the bottom and sides of plate. Flute edges with floured fingers. Add water to evaporated milk to make 1 cup and whisk with eggs until well mixed. Sprinkle canned vegetables on the crust. Flake the ham and sprinkle on vegetables, then add onion and cheese. Pour the egg mixture over all and bake at 375°F about 45 minutes, or until quiche tests done. (The filling should be set—like custard, the edges of the crust should be golden brown, and a knife inserted near the center should come out clean. Do not overcook.) Let stand a few minutes, then cut into wedges. Serves 4 to 6.

Pasta Primavera

Canned vegetables are no substitute for fresh, especially in a pasta primavera. Still, this version makes a brave showing when you're forced to make a meal from your emergency shelf. If you can add a handful of fresh broccoli or snap peas, of course, they'll make it that much better.

1 clove garlic, halved
1 28-ounce can tomatoes, drained and chopped
1 8-ounce can carrots and peas, drained
1 8-ounce can cut green beans, drained
1 4-ounce can sliced mushrooms, drained

1 small onion, minced
about 12 pitted black olives, sliced
1/3 cup virgin olive oil
3 tablespoons red wine vinegar
2 teaspoons mixed Italian seasonings
16 ounces linguine or other pasta, cooked al dente

Rub a serving bowl well with garlic, then put garlic and the rest of the vegetables in a roomy pan. Toss with vinegar and oil and heat gently. Discard garlic. Place hot pasta in serving bowl, toss with vegetable mixture, and serve at once. Serves 6 to 8.

Pass grated Parmesan or Romano cheese, add soft breadsticks, butter, and a robust red wine.

Sixteen

Saucy and Smart

Pineapple Salsa

This spicy and unusual sauce will make any plain grilled meat or fish sit up and whistle Dixie. It's especially good with meaty fish, such as tuna and swordfish, and grilled chicken or pork.

2 tablespoons oil
1 small onion, diced
1 teaspoon curry powder
2 tablespoons minced fresh ginger root
$^1/_2$ jalapeño pepper, minced
1 18-ounce can crushed pineapple, with juice

Sauté onion, curry powder, ginger, and jalapeño in hot oil until onion is just tender. Stir in pineapple with juice and bring to a boil until everything is well blended and thoroughly hot. Serve warm or cold. Makes $2^1/_2$ cups.

Microwave Cheese Sauce Supreme

This velvety cheese sauce was developed by the Wisconsin Milk Marketing Board. You can make this at home in batches to warm up aboard in the microwave. It keeps up to a week in the refrigerator.

1 cup milk
2 tablespoons instant-blend flour
2 tablespoons butter
1 cup grated cheddar
salt, pepper to taste

Combine ingredients in a 4-cup bowl and microwave on High, stirring every 30 seconds, until thick and smooth. Makes 1½ cups.

Serve on vegetables or meat, or combine with 8 ounces cooked macaroni to make a main dish.

Foolproof White Sauce

This is the base for sauces (add herbs), creamed dishes (add dried chipped beef or chopped hard-boiled eggs), and many casseroles (in place of condensed cream soups).

1 cup cold milk
2 tablespoons instant-blend flour
dash salt
dash pepper
2 tablespoons butter

Stir everything but butter together in a small saucepan, then cook, stirring, over low-medium heat until thick and smooth. Stir in butter. Makes 1¼ cups.

To microwave, combine ingredients in a 4-cup microware container and cook on High, turning and stirring every 30 seconds, until thick and smooth.

sauces

Gringo Green Sauce

1 10-ounce package frozen chopped spinach, thawed and drained
$1/2$ cup chopped parsley
$1/2$ teaspoon dill weed
3 scallions, diced
1 cup mayonnaise
garlic salt to taste

Press spinach between paper towels to remove any excess moisture. Combine everything in a bowl (for a smoother sauce, use a food processor), adding garlic salt to taste. Serve over hot vegetables or as a dip with crackers or raw vegetables. Makes 2 cups.

Green Sauce with a Kick

The blend of herbs in this versatile sauce is intoxicatingly delicious, and it gets better if flavors are allowed to chill and mingle overnight. Serve over hot or cold seafood, cold cuts, boiled shrimp, or even a plain or cheese omelet. You do need a blender or food processor to make it, so if you don't have either on board, make this sauce at home to use along the way. It keeps several days in the refrigerator.

1 cup tightly packed parsley sprigs
1 cup tightly packed watercress leaves
1 cup tightly packed basil leaves
$1/4$ cup pine nuts or toasted almonds
$1/4$ cup freshly squeezed lime juice
$1/4$ cup olive oil
2 teaspoons minced garlic
$1/2$ teaspoon Tabasco

Process all ingredients until smooth, cover, and chill 24 hours. Stir before using. Makes 1 cup.

Pecan Fudge Sauce

Make up a couple of batches of this nutty sauce at home and seal them in boilable bags. Refrigerate up to two weeks. To heat, place bags in hot water. Serve the warm sauce over plain cake, ice cream, or canned pudding.

$1/4$ cup water
3 tablespoons cornstarch
1 cup light corn syrup
$1/4$ cup brown sugar, firmly packed
1 teaspoon vanilla
1 teaspoon imitation rum flavor
2 tablespoons butter
$1/2$ cup broken pecans

In a small saucepan stir the water into the cornstarch, then add the syrup and brown sugar. Cook over low flame, stirring constantly, until it thickens. Stir in flavorings, butter, and pecans. Serve at once or refrigerate for future use. Makes $1\frac{1}{4}$ cups.

Butterscotch Sauce

This sauce transforms canned pears or a plain pound cake into a gourmet dessert.

1 4-serving package instant butterscotch pudding mix
$3/4$ cup light corn syrup
$2/3$ cup evaporated milk
water to thin

In a medium bowl combine pudding mix, syrup, and milk and whisk thoroughly. Let stand about 10 minutes, until it thickens, then whisk in a little water to achieve desired consistency. Makes $1\frac{1}{2}$ cups.

Seventeen

Sweet Somethings: Desserts

H ere are some sweet dreams to end your meals—indoors and out. Enjoy the fancy recipes, but don't forget those old standbys, marshmallows toasted over the campfire. Melty and warm, flavored with a whisper of wood smoke, and basking in the glow of good company and a flickering fire, they are still one of life's most sumptuous desserts.

Dessert Fun-Do

8 ounces cream cheese, at room temperature
1 7-ounce jar marshmallow cream
^{1}/4 cup orange juice
2 tablespoons fresh orange zest
fresh fruit (strawberries, banana and pineapple chunks, apple wedges)

Beat cream cheese with marshmallow cream, orange juice, and orange zest. Makes 1^1/2 cups.

Put the Fun-Do in the center of the table, surrounded by fresh fruit or chunks of angel food cake. Each person spears a chunk with a fork and dips it into the sauce. Tradition dictates that if you drop your dipper in the sauce, you must kiss everyone at the table.

Deep South Banana Pudding

Although this has been a Southern standard for years, it may be new to you. As it chills, the wafers soften and everything blends into creamy, flavorful goo. Vanilla wafers and instant pudding are available in regular and sugar-free versions.

2 cups regular or nonfat milk
1 4-serving package instant vanilla pudding mix
3 ripe, firm bananas, sliced*
36 vanilla wafers
1 quart whipped topping

Beat milk and pudding mix together in a container that will hold at least 2 quarts. Remove 1 cup of the pudding and cover remainder with a layer of sliced bananas, a layer of wafers, and a layer of whipped topping. Repeat layers, and finish with the rest of the pudding. Spread to edges to seal. Cover and refrigerate several hours or overnight. Serves 8 to 10.

*Banana slices are less likely to brown if they're dipped in lemon juice or Fruit-Fresh.

Cold Oven Cookies

These quick cookie squares require no baking. They hold together better if they're cold, so make them on a chilly day or keep them in the refrigerator.

2 cups graham cracker crumbs
16 ounces powdered sugar
1 16-ounce jar peanut butter
$\frac{1}{2}$ stick butter, melted
16 ounces real chocolate chips, melted

Combine cracker crumbs, powdered sugar, and peanut butter in a 9-by-11-inch pan and drizzle with butter. (Melt butter in the microwave or in a double boiler, using a container large enough to hold the chocolate chips you'll melt later.) Mix thoroughly, then pat firmly into the pan in an even layer. Chill. Melt chocolate chips and spread over crumb layer. Chill, then cut into 16 to 18 squares.

desserts

Uncookies

These easy cookies are best made with square white sandwich bread. Cut off the crusts if you want to be fancy; I don't bother.

about 10 slices white sandwich bread
1 14-ounce can sweetened condensed milk
2 cups sweetened flaked coconut

Cut each slice of bread into 4 strips. Pour sweetened condensed milk into a shallow dish and fill another dish with coconut. Dip bread in milk, then coat well with coconut. Bake on a well-greased cookie sheet at 375°F for 15 to 20 minutes or until the "cookies" are golden brown. Makes about 40 cookies.

Work-of-the-Devil Pie

Idle hands make sweet work in this sinfully rich and slothfully easy pie. It forms its own fudgy crust, making the cook look like a miracle worker in mere minutes. Serve it slathered with whipped cream or whipped topping. It's so dark and chocolaty, it really needs the contrast of a light, white, whipped topping.

1 stick butter	1 cup sugar
2 squares semisweet chocolate	splash vanilla
2 eggs	dash salt
$1/2$ cup flour	$1/2$ teaspoon instant coffee

Preheat oven to 350°F and melt butter in a pie plate. Add chocolate and return plate to oven just until chocolate melts. Whisk eggs until light, then add to butter mixture with remaining ingredients. Mix well. Bake at 350°F for 25 to 30 minutes. Let cool at least 20 minutes before cutting. Serves 6.

desserts

Nice-and-Slice Cookies

Whip up this dough on board or at home any time you're in the mood. The dough can wait up to 10 days in the refrigerator or up to 90 days in the freezer. When you're ready to bake, slice and bake only as many cookies as you want each time. The cookies are best if made with real butter.

2 sticks butter
2 cups brown sugar, firmly packed
2 eggs
1 teaspoon vanilla
3 1/3 cups flour
1 teaspoon baking soda
1 cup finely chopped nuts, mini chocolate chips, or flaked coconut

Beat butter and sugar together until light, then beat in eggs and vanilla. Combine dry ingredients and stir in, then stir in the nuts, chocolate chips, or coconut. On a floured towel, shape the dough into 3 logs. Wrap individually in plastic wrap and chill 4 hours or more. To bake, slice about 1/4 inch thick and bake on ungreased cookie sheets at 375°F for 5 or 6 minutes or until set and lightly browned on the edges. Cool thoroughly on wire racks before storing in tightly sealed containers. Makes 36 cookies.

Raspberry Chocolate Torte

1 loaf-size pound cake
1 10-ounce jar raspberry preserves
1 14-ounce can chocolate frosting

Using a sharp bread knife, carefully cut pound cake into 4 layers. Spread 2 with preserves, 1 with frosting, and assemble cake. Frost top and sides with remaining chocolate frosting. Serves 8 to 10.

desserts

Flaming Bananas

This is one of the easiest desserts to make, yet because it is flamed, it adds a fancy finale to the meal.

10 firm bananas
2 tablespoons lemon juice
$1/2$ cup sweetened flaked coconut
$1/3$ cup sugar
$1/2$ cup cognac or rum

Peel bananas and nestle them in a buttered shallow casserole. Sprinkle with lemon juice, coconut, and sugar. Bake at 350°F until bananas are brown but not mushy. Heat cognac or rum in a shallow skillet, pour over bananas, and light with a match. Serves 10.

Coffee Custard

1 tablespoon cornstarch
2 cups milk
$3/4$ cup light corn syrup
2 eggs
1 cup strong, hot coffee

In a paper cup add just enough milk to the cornstarch to make a thin paste. Over low heat (milk scorches easily) heat remaining milk and corn syrup to boiling. Beat eggs and stir them, the hot coffee, and the cornstarch mixture into milk mixture. Cook over low flame, stirring constantly, until it thickens. Pour into individual dishes and chill. Serves 4 to 5.

Gingerbread A-Go-Go

Because this recipe calls for corn syrup and oil, you don't have to cream shortening and sugar. It's easy to mix by hand.

desserts

1 cup brown sugar, firmly
    packed
1 cup light or dark corn syrup
$^1/_2$ cup salad oil
3 cups flour
1 tablespoon ground ginger
1 teaspoon ground cloves
1 teaspoon baking soda

1 cup milk, soured with
    1 teaspoon vinegar or
    lemon juice
applesauce, canned vanilla
    pudding, whipped cream,
    or canned vanilla frosting
    for topping

In a roomy saucepan, heat sugar and corn syrup until sugar dissolves. Turn off heat and stir in oil. Shake dry ingredients together in a bag and mix into the sugar mixture, then add sour milk. Turn into a buttered 9-by-13-inch pan and bake at 350°F for 25 to 30 minutes or until springy to the touch. Serve warm with your choice of topping. Cut into 12 squares.

Eggless Cake

This is a "hard times" recipe that has been around since my grand-mother's day. Its advantage for the RV cook is that it can be made without eggs and without a beater.

1 cup water
$^1/_3$ cup shortening
1 cup brown sugar, firmly
    packed
2 teaspoons apple pie spice
$^1/_2$ cup chopped, pitted dates
2 cups raisins

1 teaspoon baking soda
    dissolved in 1 tablespoon
    water
$^1/_2$ teaspoon baking powder
2 cups flour
vanilla frosting (canned or
    homemade)

In a roomy saucepan, bring water, shortening, sugar, apple pie spice, dates, and raisins to a boil, then boil for 3 minutes. Cool. Stir baking soda mixture, baking powder, and flour into fruit mixture. Turn into an 8-inch square pan and bake at 350°F for about 30 minutes or until springy to the touch. Cool, then frost. Cut into 9 squares.

desserts

Trifling Trifle

2 individually packaged jelly rolls (e.g., Little Debbie brand)
2 tablespoons sherry (optional)
2 cups milk
1 4-serving package instant vanilla pudding mix

Cut each jelly roll into 4 slices and divide among dessert dishes. Or press them into clear glass or plastic drinking glasses, so they'll show through. Drizzle with sherry, if desired. Shake milk and pudding mix together in a clean jar and pour into the dishes. Chill until serving time. Serves 4.

Cold-Oven Peanut Butter Squares

Various recipes for boiled cookies have been around for years. In this version, the boiled batter is put into a pan and cut into squares, like fudge.

1 cup sugar
1 stick butter
$^1/_2$ cup water
2 teaspoons vanilla
$2^1/_2$ cups rolled oats
2 tablespoons powdered milk
$^1/_2$ cup peanut butter

Mix sugar, butter, and water in a saucepan and bring to a full boil, then boil for 30 seconds. Remove from heat and mix in remaining ingredients. Working quickly, spread mixture into a buttered 8-inch square pan and cool. Cut into 9 squares.

Don't forget: When camping at high altitudes, all cooking times are longer.

Cookie Crumb Cake

This is another cake that's easy to store and carry because it's not frosted. It's a good way to use up those odds and ends of cookies that get stale so quickly in the outdoor life. Just put them in a heavy-duty plastic bag, then crush them with a rolling pin.

1 box yellow cake mix (to make 2 layers)	*Glaze*
2 cups cookie or graham cracker crumbs	1 cup powdered sugar
³/₄ cup brown sugar, firmly packed	¹/₂ teaspoon vanilla
¹/₂ cup chopped walnuts	1 to 2 tablespoons water
1 teaspoon cinnamon	

Prepare cake batter according to package directions and pour half into a greased 9-by-13-inch pan. Combine crumbs, sugar, nuts, and cinnamon and sprinkle half over batter in pan. Carefully add rest of batter and top with remaining crumb mixture. Bake at 350°F for about 45 minutes or until it tests done. While it cools, mix together glaze ingredients, adding enough water to make a thin frosting. Drizzle over the cake. Serves 12 to 15.

desserts

Bananas in a Cloud

6 ripe bananas	¹/₂ teaspoon apple pie spice
1 tablespoon lemon juice	¹/₃ cup water
1 cup light corn syrup	1 aerosol can real whipped cream
1 cup sugar	

Cut bananas in half lengthwise, then into chunks, and toss lightly with lemon juice. Bring corn syrup, sugar, apple pie spice, and water to a boil. Remove from heat, cool, and gently fold in the bananas. Make a "nest" of whipped cream in individual dishes and spoon on banana mixture. Serves 6.

Drizzletops

This is a devious recipe, because it's an easy way to put a homemade frill on a store-bought dessert. To make it work, you need either a small roasting bag or one of the boilable bags sold for use with meal-seal appliances.

3 ounces semisweet chocolate
1 tablespoon butter
store-bought cookies or cake

Place chocolate and butter in boilable bag and lower into simmering water until melted. Using an oven mitt, squeeze bag gently to mix well, dipping in the hot water as necessary. Arrange cookies or cake close together (on waxed paper to catch drips) so you can sweep across the lineup with an unbroken motion. Working quickly, snip a tiny corner from the bottom of the bag so it will leak a small stream of melted chocolate. Then zigzag it across the dessert. When you have squeezed out the last of the chocolate, throw the bag away. Makes about $\frac{1}{3}$ cup.

Zero-Calorie Desserts

Well, OK, they're not 100 percent noncaloric, but they do pack all the punch of sweet desserts with only the barest few calories. If you're diabetic, check with your dietician for exchange values. Many desserts, such as sugar-free gelatins and soft drinks, are "free" exchanges. In any case, be aware that sugar substitutes are controversial and are not for everyone.

In making most desserts, I use the small, covered plastic containers that hold $\frac{1}{2}$ cup each. The lids fit tightly so I don't have to worry about spills in the RV refrigerator, and portions are premeasured for the dieter. This is especially helpful if you have only one person in the family who needs special desserts.

In the diet foods section of the supermarket you'll find whipped topping that is creamy, delicious, and almost "free." With one crushed dietetic cookie you can add a crumb topping to an otherwise plain diet dessert, or crush dietetic hard candies to create a tangy "sugar sprinkle" for an added burst of flavor. Or top each serving of diet pudding with one pecan or almond half for texture contrast. The "cost" to the dieter is peanuts.

If you're on a strict diet, be sure to read labels. Some so-called dietetic or diabetic foods are sugar-free but are high in saturated fats, fructose, and other nutrients that must be "charged" to your "account."

Apricot Cream Surprise

1 4-serving package sugar-free instant vanilla pudding
1/4 teaspoon cinnamon
2 cups skim milk
1 4- to 7-ounce jar baby food strained apricots

Whisk pudding mix, cinnamon, and milk together. Divide into 5 dishes or containers and place a dollop of apricots in the center of each.
Variations: Instead of baby food apricots, try baby food apple-blueberry dessert, applesauce, or strained pears.

Seafoam

1 13-ounce can evaporated skim milk
1 package sugar-free lime gelatin
1/2 cup boiling water

Pour milk into any shallow tray and freeze just until ice crystals begin to form. Dissolve gelatin in water and chill until it's the consistency of egg white. Whip milk and gelatin together with an electric beater on high until foamy and stiff. Pour into 6 containers and chill until firm.

Ginger Peachy

1 packet unflavored gelatin
1/2 cup water
2 cups sugar-free ginger ale

1 8-ounce can peaches, sugar-free pack, drained (juice may be added to water measurement)

Soften gelatin in water, then heat gently until gelatin dissolves. Add ginger ale. Divide cut-up peaches among 6 containers, add gelatin mixture, and chill until set.

No-Fault Ambrosia

1 package sugar-free lime gelatin
1 8-ounce can crushed pineapple, drained
6 ounces nonfat cottage cheese

Combine cottage cheese and pineapple, sprinkle with gelatin, and mix well. Divide among 6 to 8 serving containers.

Save for a Rainy Day

Bring out these recipes on a day when you're weathered in and want to fuss around the galley, letting the aromas of food surround you and lift your spirits.

We've been rained in for days at a time in our RV, once during a hurricane in Nova Scotia and other times during tropical storms in Florida. During one rainy, muddy springtime in Vermont, we couldn't venture out for a week, and then only in boots and oilskins.

I set aside this section for a rainy day because these recipes are ideal for RV fun, although they're not shortcut quickies. You can fuss over them, enjoying the process as much as the product.

Make a skillet upside-down cake. Arrange pineapple slices in melted butter in a heavy 8-inch skillet. Sprinkle with brown sugar, then drizzle with a bottle of shake-and-pour pancake mix, mixed according to directions on the label after adding 1 tablespoon of sugar and a pinch of cinnamon. Cover and cook over low flame until the batter is springy and set.

desserts

Popcorn Balls

First, butter everything that will come in contact with the sticky mess that will result. You'll need a pair of clean rubber or plastic gloves to protect your hands while you form the balls. Butter the gloves, too.

12 cups popped corn,
   unpopped kernels removed
1 16-ounce package marsh-
   mallows
½ stick butter

1 cup gumdrops, chopped
   nuts, chocolate chips,
   or butterscotch chips
   (optional)

Put popcorn in a big buttered container and keep warm in a 250°F oven. In a heavy pan over very low heat, or in the microwave, heat marshmallows and butter together until melted and smooth. Pour over popcorn and mix well with a buttered spoon. Add one of the optional ingredients, if using, and shape gently into balls. Don't pack too tightly. Wrap individually in waxed paper or plastic wrap. Makes 12 to 15 popcorn balls.

This can also be turned into a family sculpture game if you have buttered gloves for all players. (I carry disposable plastic gloves aboard and use them for all sorts of messy tasks, from greasing wheel bearings to handling raw bacon.) Instead of forming popcorn balls, have everyone make an animal, something seasonal like a Christmas tree or a shamrock, or whatever suits their fancy. What with the shaping and trimming, the job can fill a happy hour.

desserts

For fitness' sake, get your family into the "walking dessert" habit. Pass out shiny apples, licorice whips, all-day suckers, Tootsie Pops, popcorn balls, granola bars, or other individual treats. Or double-time to the campground store and buy a round of Popsicles or lollipops for all.

Place a layer of sliced bananas in a buttered pie plate and sprinkle with lemon juice, sugar (or equivalent), and a little cinnamon. Drizzle with squeeze margarine and top with a solid layer of marshmallows. Bake at 350°F until marshmallows are browned and puffy.

Crêpes Grand Marnier

Few foods are more versatile than crêpes, which can be filled with almost anything and served for breakfast, lunch, dinner, snacks, and desserts. The drawback is that it takes a long time to make crêpes one at a time. A rainy day is the perfect time to stow away a stock of crêpes.

Stack them with paper towels or waxed paper between, then refrigerate or freeze for future use. Or make this triple batch of festive dessert crêpes. They'll keep for a couple of weeks in the refrigerator.

6 eggs	Filling
2 cups milk	1 stick butter, at room temperature
2 tablespoons melted butter	
1 $^{1}/_{2}$ cups flour	1 cup sifted powdered sugar
2 tablespoons sugar	$^{3}/_{4}$ cup orange juice
	$^{3}/_{4}$ cup honey or light corn syrup
	$^{1}/_{2}$ cup orange liqueur
	1 orange, thinly sliced in quarters

To make crêpes, whisk together eggs and milk and stir in butter, flour, and sugar. Cover and refrigerate 2 hours. Using a scant $^{1}/_{4}$ cup each time, pour batter into a hot, lightly sprayed, 8-inch nonstick skillet and tilt quickly so that batter flows around the bottom of the pan to form a thin pancake. When it's golden on the bottom, turn and cook the other side. Makes 24 crêpes.

To make filling, combine butter and sugar and carefully spread each crêpe with the mixture. Fold into quarters and stack in refrigerator containers in whatever size batches you can use. Combine orange juice and corn syrup in a small saucepan, bring to a boil, reduce heat, and add orange slices. Stir in liqueur and divide among the containers of crêpes. To

desserts

serve, gently warm the syrupy crêpes in the microwave and spoon onto serving plates.

For a flaming dessert, heat about ¼ cup orange liqueur in a small pan or skillet, pour over crêpes, and light with a match.

Butter Rum Fudge

2 cups dark brown sugar,
  firmly packed
1 cup white sugar
1 stick butter
1 cup half and half
1 7-ounce jar marshmallow
  cream

12 ounces butterscotch chips
1 cup dried apricots, snipped
  into bits
1 cup chopped nuts
1 ½ teaspoons butter-rum-
  vanilla flavoring*

Combine sugars, butter, and half and half in a roomy saucepan (at least 3-quart capacity). Stirring constantly, bring to a boil over medium heat until it forms a soft ball when a drop is placed in cold water. (If you have a candy thermometer, it should read 238°F.) Remove from heat and stir in marshmallow cream, butterscotch chips, apricots, nuts, and flavoring. Beat well and spread in a buttered 8-inch square pan. Cool and cut into squares as large or small as you choose.

*If you can't find this flavoring, substitute 1 teaspoon rum flavor, ½ teaspoon vanilla, and ½ teaspoon butter flavoring.

Fast Lane

◆ Make a quick pie crust by combining 1¾ cups rolled oats, ½ cup flour, ⅓ cup firmly packed brown sugar, and ⅓ cup melted butter. Press into a pie pan, reserving ⅓ cup of the mixture for a topping, and bake 15 minutes at 350°F. Cool and fill with instant pudding, canned apple pie filling, or your favorite refrigerator cheesecake recipe. Sprinkle with reserved oats mixture and chill.

◆ Empty a can of applesauce into a pie plate or shallow casserole, sprinkle with sugar and cinnamon, and top with a meringue made by beating 2 egg whites with ¼ cup sugar. Bake at 375°F about 15 minutes or until meringue is set and browned.

◆ Make a canned fruit dessert more festive and lower in calories by pouring off the heavy syrup and saucing the fruit with a fizzy diet soda.

◆ Make a tangy topping for gingerbread or spice cake by whisking together 1 cup plain yogurt, juice of 1 small lemon, and 1 can sweetened condensed milk. Mix and spread quickly. Mixture will set like custard.

◆ Fill an unbaked pie shell with your choice of ready-to-bake cookie dough and bake at 350°F until crust is browned and the dough is done through. Serve in wedges.

◆ Add a banana to your favorite bread pudding recipe before baking. Serve warm with milk or cream.

◆ Consider serving a dessert coffee or tea. Simply add a couple of tablespoons of liqueur to each cup. Almond or raspberry liqueur goes well with tea; brandies and cognacs are good with coffee.

desserts

Eighteen

Gifts That Say "Good-Bye and Godspeed"

O ne of the joys of camping is meeting so many nice people. Campground neighbors form quick friendships, but then the gladness
turns to good-byes as we go our separate ways. In some cases, we may
correspond with families later, or we may even conspire to meet again
along the way. In rare instances, we meet again by chance. Usually, however, only the warm memories are left.

One way to keep the thread of friendship alive a little longer is to send
along a food gift with the traveler. Food gifts are inexpensive and personal, and they can be given without fanfare or a feeling of obligation.
Here are some food gifts that are practical to give (and to receive).

Galliano Cocoa Mix

*Unlike the powdered drink mix on the next page, this one is a buttery
paste that should be stored in the refrigerator. It will keep for up to four
weeks, so make a single or double batch at home and carry it aboard to bring
out in camp. To share it, portion it into pretty paper cups, wrap in plastic,
and provide these instructions: "Put 1 tablespoon of this mix in a mug, fill
with very hot milk, coffee, or tea and stir. Refrigerate unused mix and use
promptly." Use real butter, not margarine.*

2 sticks butter, at room
    temperature
4 cups brown sugar, firmly
    packed
$^2/_3$ cup Galliano liqueur

$^1/_2$ teaspoon almond flavor
$^1/_2$ teaspoon vanilla flavor
$^1/_2$ cup powdered creamer
2 teaspoons pumpkin pie spice

Beat butter and sugar, then add in the other ingredients until everything is smooth and well blended. Pack into a clean, lidded container(s) and keep cold. Makes about 6 cups mix.

Truffles

These are best made when the weather isn't too hot and steamy, so tuck away the ingredients and bring them out on a cool day when you need a family project. Arranged on a pretty paper plate, they make a beautiful calling card when you are meeting new campground neighbors.

18 ounces real chocolate chips
1 14-ounce can sweetened condensed milk
1 tablespoon vanilla
finely chopped nuts, grated coconut, chocolate jimmies, etc.

Melt chocolate chips in the sweetened condensed milk in the microwave for about 3 minutes, stirring every 30 seconds. Careful! Chocolate scorches easily. Stir in vanilla and chill until firm and fudgy, about an hour. Shape into walnut-size balls and roll in nuts, coconut, or sprinkles. Makes about 18 truffles.

Caravan Cocoa Latte Mix

Simply bag this in any amounts you want to give away, in zip-top plastic bags trimmed with bright stickers and a label of instructions: "Put 2 tablespoons of this mixture into a cup, then fill with boiling water and stir."

gifts

2 cups sugar
16 ounces powdered creamer
2 cups powdered milk
1 cup unsweetened cocoa
$1/2$ cup instant coffee
1 teaspoon cinnamon

Shake everything together in a big plastic bag until it's well mixed. Divide into smaller bags and seal well. Makes 7 cups mix.

Ladybugs

These are fun to make, and children can help. Plan ahead to have all the supplies on board. Buy the spices in bulk at a specialty shop when you see them on sale; they're much more expensive in small supermarket packages.

Give these instructions with each bug: "To make mulled cider, drop this ladybug into 6 cups of apple juice, simmer 30 minutes, then strain into mugs. (Discard the bug. Whole spices could be harmful if swallowed.) Sip and enjoy!"

6 oranges, halved
about 2 cups brown sugar, firmly packed
12 cinnamon sticks
12 whole nutmegs
24 whole allspice
96 whole cloves

Dig the "meat" out of the oranges to use in fruit salad. Bake the orange shells on a rack, cut side up, at 250°F for about 2 hours, until they're leathery. After they cool, pack each tightly with brown sugar. Press spices into sugar to make a "bug," with a cinnamon stick for the body, 2 allspice eyes, a nutmeg head, and 8 clove legs. Wrap each bug tightly in plastic wrap and store in the refrigerator. They'll keep indefinitely if the orange shells were dried out enough. Makes 12 ladybugs.

gifts

My Own Mustard

Conjure up a big batch of this zesty spread and divide into clean jars. Be sure to tell recipients to store it in the refrigerator and used within a month.

$^{2}/_{3}$ cup dry mustard
$^{1}/_{2}$ cup sugar
8 eggs, beaten
1 cup vinegar (experiment with different kinds)
$^{1}/_{2}$ cup dry white wine
1 teaspoon thyme
1 teaspoon basil
1 teaspoon oregano
1 teaspoon dill weed

In a saucepan large enough to hold double the volume of this mixture, combine mustard and sugar, then stir in eggs, vinegar, and wine. Cook over low heat, beating continuously, until it foams up and becomes thick. It will double in size, then return to its original volume. Stir in herbs, cool, stir, and pour into clean jars. Cover and refrigerate. Makes about 4 cups.

Chutney Cheese Crock

This is a delicious way to use up bits of leftover cheese. It makes a pretty gift when packed into clear plastic cups and topped with a layer of chopped almonds. Store in the refrigerator but serve at room temperature, with crackers.

16 ounces cream cheese, at room temperature
2 tablespoons butter, at room temperature
2 cups grated yellow cheese (cheddar or whatever you have)
$^{1}/_{2}$ cup chutney
3 tablespoons dry sherry
1 teaspoon curry powder
$^{1}/_{2}$ cup chopped, roasted almonds (plus more for topping)

gifts

Beat cream cheese and butter in a large mixing bowl, then combine with other ingredients until everything is well mixed. Pack into containers and top with a layer of chopped nuts. Makes 4 cups.

Spiced Almonds

Almonds are economical when bought in bulk and are one of nature's most elegant foods. Make up a huge batch of these toothsome nuts and package some in zip-top plastic bags for sharing.

2 cups sugar
2 teaspoons cinnamon
dash nutmeg
1 cup water
1 tablespoon butter
2 teaspoons vanilla
4 cups raw or roasted almonds

Boil sugar, spices, and water, stirring occasionally, until mixture reaches the soft ball stage, or 238°F on a candy thermometer. Remove from heat and stir in butter and vanilla, then stir in nuts. Working quickly, turn out mixture onto waxed paper, spreading and separating to form as thin a layer as possible. Let cool completely, then break up into small chunks of 1 to 2 nuts each and seal in bags in giftable batches.

gifts

Bloody Shame

This zippy vegetable-juice cocktail can be used as a base for Bloody Marys or enjoyed in its nonalcoholic state. It's best made a day ahead to allow flavors to blend. The secret to its tang is freshly squeezed lemon juice. Give away by the quart or pint with instructions to serve over ice with a celery stalk swizzle, with or without a shot of vodka.

2 46-ounce cans tomato or V-8 juice
1 cup freshly squeezed lemon or lime juice
2 tablespoons Worcestershire sauce
salt, pepper, hot sauce to taste
1 teaspoon celery salt

Combine all ingredients and portion into bottles. Cover and chill thoroughly. Makes about 3 quarts.

Canny Nutbread

Rinse and dry 12- to 16-ounce tin cans and recycle them as disposable baking pans. Wrap and chill this bread for easier slicing, and serve in thin slices for tea time or a bedtime snack.

1 stick butter	$1/3$ cup milk
1 cup honey	a total of $1^1/2$ cups raisins,
2 eggs	chopped dates, and chopped
2 cups flour	nuts in any combination
2 teaspoons baking powder	

Cream butter and honey and beat in eggs. Add flour and baking powder to creamed mixture alternately with milk, beating well after each addition. Fold in dried fruit and nuts. Spoon into lightly greased tins, filling each no more than $2/3$ full, and bake at 350°F for 30 to 35 minutes or until loaves test done with a toothpick. For easiest removal, let loaves cool in the tins, then remove bottoms with a can opener and push out the bread. Makes 4 can-size loaves.

Cheerio!

What a cheery way to say "Cheerio" to your new friends. Send them off with a box of these goodies to munch along the highway.

28 soft caramel candies
1 tablespoon water
4 cups round oat cereal

Combine caramels and water in a microwave container and cook at Medium power, stirring every 30 seconds, until melted and smooth. Put cereal in a buttered bowl and pour on caramel mixture, tossing quickly until everything is evenly coated. Rinse hands in cold water and shape mixture into 1-inch balls. Arrange on waxed paper until set, then transfer to pretty paper plates for giving. Makes 24 candies.

Popcakes

6 cups popped corn, unpopped kernels removed	$^1/_2$ cup sugar
1 cup peanuts	$^1/_2$ cup light corn syrup
$^1/_2$ cup raisins	$^1/_2$ cup peanut butter
	$^1/_2$ teaspoon vanilla

Do not salt or butter popcorn. Toss with peanuts and raisins in a big buttered bowl. In a small saucepan bring sugar and corn syrup to a foamy boil, then remove from heat and stir in peanut butter and vanilla. Mix with popcorn. Press mixture into a buttered 9-by-13-inch pan and cool until firm. Cut into 12 to 15 squares and place each in a cupcake paper for serving or giving.

Poor Man's Pâté

This is most easily prepared in a food processor but can also be mashed together by hand. Use clear plastic cups for gift giving.

1 envelope unflavored gelatin
2 cups boiling water, in separate cups
2 teaspoons beef bouillon granules
1 pound liverwurst, at room temperature
8 ounces cream cheese, at room temperature
1 small onion, minced
1 tablespoon chopped parsley
pepper to taste
1 cup cold water
$^1/_3$ cup sherry or cognac

gifts

Sprinkle gelatin into 1 cup boiling water and bouillon granules into the other cup. Stir both to dissolve. Mix together liverwurst, cream cheese, onion, parsley, and pepper, making as smooth a mixture as possible. Stir in gelatin and bouillon mixtures, cold water, and sherry and pour into individual jars or cups for giving or serving. Chill. Serve with crackers or party rye bread. Makes about 6 cups.

Pick-Up-and-Go Fudge

1 cup light corn syrup
$2/3$ cup evaporated milk
16 ounces semisweet chocolate
1 tablespoon vanilla
$1^1/2$ cups sifted powdered sugar
$2/3$ cup creamy peanut butter

Line a 9-by-13-inch pan with plastic wrap, using enough sheets to cover bottom and sides completely. Spray lightly with nonstick cooking spray. In a roomy, heavy saucepan, stir together corn syrup and milk over very low heat, adding chocolate and stirring constantly until chocolate melts. Remove from heat and stir in vanilla and sugar, then beat with a spoon until smooth. Stir in peanut butter just enough to mix and marble. Spread into lined pan. Chill until firm, then turn out of the pan, peel off plastic wrap, and cut into small squares. Makes 2 pounds.

gifts

Appendix

Food Storage Guidelines

Food Item	Time Limit	How to Store
baking powder, baking soda	18 months	tightly sealed
bouillon	12 months	dry, tightly sealed
boxed foods	dated	cool, dry, safe from bugs
butter	4 weeks	as cool as possible
cake mix	12 months	cool, dry
commercially canned goods	12 months	cool, dry, rustproof
cereals	dated	dry
cheese, hard	3 to 4 months	cool, dry
cheese, soft	1 to 2 weeks	refrigerated
coconut, canned	12 to 18 months	tightly sealed; use immediately after opening or refrigerate
eggs	21 days	refrigerated or sealed
fish	1 to 2 days	refrigerated
flour, all purpose	15 months	dry, safe from bugs
flour, freshly ground	—	use immediately after grinding
flour, whole wheat	6 months	cool, dry, tightly sealed
fruit, dried	up to 1 year	cool, tightly sealed
herbs, dried	1 year	cool, dry, tightly sealed
honey	indefinitely	tightly sealed; heat if solidifies
jam, jelly	1 to 2 years	tightly sealed; use quickly after opening
meats (cold cuts)	1 to 2 days	refrigerated
meats, frozen	up to 1 year	frozen
meats, processed (ham, bacon, etc.)	1 to 2 months	frozen
meats, roasts and large cuts	up to 5 days	refrigerated
nonfat powdered milk	6 months	cool, dry

Food Item	Time Limit	How to Store
olive oil	2 years	tightly sealed, away from bright light
pastas	1 year	cool, dry, safe from bugs
peanut butter	6 months	cool, tightly sealed; use quickly after opening
pickles	1 year	tightly sealed; use quickly after opening
poultry, pieces	1 to 2 days	refrigerated
poultry, whole	9 to 12 months	frozen
rice, brown	up to 15 years in nitrogen-pack cans	tightly sealed; use within 2 weeks after opening
rice, white	indefinitely	cool, dry, safe from bugs
shortening	6 months	cool, dark, tightly sealed
sugar, brown	3 to 4 months	tightly sealed
sugar, white	indefinitely	cool, dry, tightly sealed
wheat berries	indefinitely	tightly sealed
vegetable oil	1 year	cool, dark, tightly sealed
yeast	dated	cool

* *Home-canned, pickled, and preserved items may not last as long as commercial products.*

* *These times apply to items stored at normal home temperatures. Food should not be left for long periods in an RV that sits outdoors or in a very hot or very cold storage yard or shed.*

Miscellaneous Tips

Baking soda is a food-quality abrasive. Use it as a cleanser, neutralizer, sweetener, and deodorizer. To clean burned-on residue from a skillet or pan, fill it with an inch of water and a tablespoon or two of baking soda. Bring to a boil for several minutes and let it cool. The soil should lift off easily.

Bottle brush. To scrub areas you can't reach otherwise, add a few drops of detergent, warm water, and some pebbles or uncooked rice. Shake to scrub.

Bulk food and freeze-dried and dehydrated food can be ordered from Nitro-Pak Preparedness Center, 800-866-4876, www.nitro-pak.com.

Butter corn evenly and quickly by dipping each ear in a pan of hot water in which you've melted a stick of butter. The butter floats to the top, coating the corn as you remove it.

Campfire soot cleans easily off the bottoms of pots if you coat them first with soft bar soap.

Dishwasher detergent plus a soak in very hot water is the best way to keep plastic containers odor-free. Keep your hands out of this harsh mixture.

Fat substitute. The Dannon people suggest using plain, nonfat yogurt in place of oil and eggs in brownie mix; the Mott folks suggest using applesauce instead of oil in cake mixes.

Folding dish drainers are found in camping and specialty catalogs. Save time and work by letting dishes air-dry.

Food safety. It's easy to remember that "life begins at 40." In terms of refrigerator safety, this means that at temperatures above 40°F, organisms begin to grow more rapidly. Use a refrigerator thermometer to be sure yours stays in the safe range.

Ice cream. I buy ice cream only by the pint, and it's almost never available in this size except in space-hogging round containers. To get around this, let it soften just enough to remove from the round tubs, press into rectangular refrigerator containers, and place in the freezer.

Lemon juice. Bottled juice doesn't have the same punch as freshly squeezed juice. When lemons or limes are on sale, use your electric juicer at home to make a quart or two of juice, and freeze in ice-cube trays. Bag the cubes and keep them in your RV freezer.

Meatballs and hamburgers look better and cook more evenly when they're all the same size. Here's an easy way to divide ground meat. After preparing your favorite meat mix with onions, breadcrumbs, or whatever, pile it onto a sheet of waxed paper and pat into a flat, even circle. Using a long knife, such as a bread knife, press through the circle to cut in half, then quarters. For more servings, as for meatballs, keep pressing the knife across the circle to continue dividing into 16ths, 32nds, etc. Then form into balls or patties.

Oven spills. Cut paper (not plastic!) drinking straws in pieces and insert them as "chimneys" in the top crust of a fruit pie. They'll prevent boilovers. When spills occur, sprinkle them heavily with salt. They'll dry hard and crispy and will be easier to remove.

Paper cups are expensive and bulky to use routinely, but keep some on hand for small mixing jobs, such as whisking together ketchup and grated horseradish to make cocktail sauce. Use paper plates for dredging fish in flour, mashing tofu, and other messy jobs.

Parsley. So many recipes call for a tablespoon or two of chopped fresh parsley. Few of us have the time and space to keep fresh herbs aboard, yet there is no real substitute for them. I buy fresh parsley by the bunch and chop large quantities at a time in the food processor or by hand. Then I pack it very lightly in small zip-top plastic bags and freeze, shaking the bags from time to time so the parsley doesn't form a solid block. One bag takes up little space in the RV freezer, and I can scoop out a tablespoon of the flaky, frozen parsley as needed.

Poison warning. Don't use an unknown wood for green-stick cooking, planking fish, or to stir a pot over the campfire. Among poisonous woods are manchineel, found in the tropics, and such shrubs as lantana and elderberry (the wood, not the berries).

Rice. Cooked rice is ideal for many dishes that require a starch base. If you make boil-in-the-bag rice, plan to cook other boilable bags at the same time, such as vegetables in butter sauce, creamed spinach, or any homemade concoction like beef Stroganoff or creamed chicken.

Rolling pin substitute. Slip a clean sock over a straight-sided glass bottle and rub with flour. For a pastry cloth alternative, use a floured linen towel (to wash, soak in *cold* water) or, for small jobs like briefly kneading biscuits, a floured paper towel.

Rubber sink mats have many other uses in the galley. Use one on the floor of the refrigerator to dampen sound, catch spills, and prevent skidding.

Self-rising flour, self-made. To make 1 cup, add $1\frac{1}{2}$ teaspoons baking powder and $\frac{1}{2}$ teaspoon salt to 1 cup less 2 teaspoons all-purpose flour.

Serve-over suggestion. When a recipe calls for a starch base (e.g., creamed chicken over biscuits) and you don't want to cook another item, serve it over rice cakes, toast, or frozen waffles warmed in the toaster. Or if you can take the salt and calories, ladle it over a bed of Chinese noodles, canned french fried onion rings, or potato sticks.

Tin-can power. Rinse cans after using, let drain, and save to use as catchalls, biscuit or cookie cutters, bread-baking tins, and disposable pans for small tasks like melting butter or heating syrup.

Tomato paste. If you often need just a teaspoon or two of tomato paste for recipes, open a can, place by dollops on a cookie sheet covered with waxed paper, and freeze. Put the frozen plops into a plastic bag and keep frozen to use as needed.

Tongs. Use a couple of spring-type wooden clothespins as handles to lift a hot grill or oven rack.

Index